SECTION LINES:
A MANITOBA ANTHOLOGY

SECTION LINES: A MANITOBA ANTHOLOGY

MARK DUNCAN, EDITOR

TURNSTONE PRESS

Turnstone Press gratefully acknowledges the assistance of the Manitoba Arts Council and the Canada Council. Special thanks to St. John's-Ravenscourt School for financial assistance.

Turnstone Press
607-100 Arthur Street
Winnipeg, Manitoba
R3B 1H3

This book was typeset by Communigraphics and printed by Hignell Printing Limited for Turnstone Press.

Printed in Canada

Cover art: *Diptych—Landscape Imprints* by Don Reichert, acrylic on paper, 44" x 30".

Cover design: Steven Rosenberg

Canadian Cataloguing in Publication Data

Main entry under title:

Section lines

ISBN 0-88801-127-X

1. Poetry, Canadian (English)—Manitoba.* 2. Poetry, Canadian (English)—20th century.* 3. Short stories, Canadian (English)—Manitoba.* 4. Canadian fiction (English)—20th century.*
I. Duncan, Mark, 1952-

PS8295.5.M3S4 1988 C811'.5'08097127 C88-098042-7
PR9198.2.M32S4 1988

for T.A.W.

My sincerest thanks to those who encouraged, criticized and helped out in a variety of ways: David Arnason, Dennis Cooley, Jamie Hutchison, Dorothy Livesay, Marilyn Morton. My special thanks to Pat Sanders for her good sense, kindness and patience; and to Wayne Tefs, who thought up the idea in the first place and wouldn't let me rest until I agreed to tackle it.

I would also like to express my gratitude to John Messenger, Headmaster of St. John's-Ravenscourt School, and the Board of Governors of SJR for their unwavering support of this project. Without their financial generosity, this book could not have been completed.

And to Jill, my wife. Thanks, sweetheart. You're the greatest.

ACKNOWLEDGEMENTS AND PERMISSIONS

ARTHUR ADAMSON:

"Spell of Trees" from *Passages of Winter*, © Arthur Adamson (Winnipeg: Turnstone Press, 1981). Reprinted by permission.

"In the House by the Prairie," © Arthur Adamson, first appeared in *Border Crossings*, Vol. 4, No. 4 (Fall 1985). Reprinted by permission.

GEORGE AMABILE:

"Canto" from *Flower and Song*, © George Amabile (Ottawa: Borealis Press Limited, 1977). Reprinted by permission.

"Churches" and "Word Games" from *Ideas of Shelter*, © George Amabile (Winnipeg: Turnstone Press, 1981). Reprinted by permission.

"Rain" from *Blood Ties*, © George Amabile (Victoria: Sono Nis Press, 1972). Reprinted by permission.

"Prairie" from *Open Country*, © George Amabile (Winnipeg: Turnstone Press, 1976). Reprinted by permission.

DAVID ARNASON:

"Sons and Fathers, Fathers and Sons" from *The Circus Performers' Bar*, © David Arnason (Vancouver: Talonbooks, 1984). Reprinted by permission.

SANDRA BIRDSELL:

"The Bride Doll" from *Ladies of the House*, © Sandra Birdsell (Winnipeg: Turnstone Press, 1984). Reprinted by permission.

KATE BITNEY:

"Noon And My Sisters" and "I Am Shown The Land" from *while you were out*, © Kate Bitney (Winnipeg: Turnstone Press, 1980). Reprinted by permission.

DI BRANDT:

"ruling his shrunken kingdom," "i wish the sky was still pasted on," "& i what do i want" and "Diana" from *questions i asked my mother*, © Di Brandt (Winnipeg: Turnstone Press, 1987). Reprinted by permission.

LOIS BRAUN:

"The Edge of the Cornfield" from *A Stone Watermelon*, © Lois Braun (Winnipeg: Turnstone Press, 1986). Reprinted by permission.

DENNIS COOLEY:

"Fielding" from *Leaving*, © Dennis Cooley (Winnipeg: Turnstone Press, 1980). Reprinted by permission.

"shapes of frost," "corvus brachyrhynchos," "by the red," "dear valentine" and "day hardens" from *Bloody Jack*, © Dennis Cooley (Winnipeg: Turnstone Press, 1984). Reprinted by permission.

"Travelling Back" from *Soul Searching*, © Dennis Cooley (Red Deer: Red Deer College Press, 1987). Reprinted by permission.

CHESTER DUNCAN:

"Up and Down in the Depression" from *Wanna Fight, Kid?*, © Chester Duncan (Winnipeg: Queenston House, 1975). Reprinted by permission.

PATRICK FRIESEN:

"he had disobeyed," "i latch the barn door," "rivers," "a silver fall," "the crouped child choking" and "now his narrow home" from *The Shunning*, © Patrick Friesen (Winnipeg: Turnstone Press, 1980). Reprinted by permission.

"terrain" from *the lands i am*, © Patrick Friesen (Winnipeg: Turnstone Press, 1976). Reprinted by permission.

"wings" from *bluebottle*, © Patrick Friesen (Winnipeg: Turnstone Press, 1978). Reprinted by permission.

"sunday afternoon" and "dream of the black river" from *Flicker and Hawk*, © Patrick Friesen (Winnipeg: Turnstone Press, 1987). Reprinted by permission.

KEITH LOUISE FULTON:

"there is no special structure women have," © Keith Louise Fulton, first appeared in *Contemporary Verse 2*, Vol. 10, No. 1 (Spring 1986). Reprinted by permission.

KRISTJANA GUNNARS:

"From Memory I," "From Memory II," "From Memory XII" and "Stefán Eyjólfsson" from *Settlement Poems 1*, © Kristjana Gunnars (Winnipeg: Turnstone Press, 1980). Reprinted by permission.

"Jóhann Briem 2, II" from *Settlement Poems 2*, © Kristjana Gunnars (Winnipeg: Turnstone Press, 1980). Reprinted by permission.

"A Long Production," © Kristjana Gunnars, first appeared in *Poetry Canada Review*, Vol. 6, No. 3 (1985). Reprinted by permission.

JAN HORNER:

"A Letter to My Mother," © Jan Horner, first appeared in *Contemporary Verse 2*, Vol. 9, No. 2 (Fall 1985). Reprinted by permission.

MARY HORODYSKI:

"Housecraft" and "At 7" from *mr. spock do you read me?*, © Mary Horodyski (Winnipeg: Turnstone Press, 1986). Reprinted by permission.

SMARO KAMBOURELI:

"Wednesday, December 21, 1980," "February 8, 1981" "February 6, 1981" and "Banff/August 5, 1981" from *in the second person*, © Smaro Kamboureli (Edmonton: Longspoon Press, 1985). Reprinted by permission.

ROBERT KROETSCH:

"Syllogisms of Desire" and "Projected Visit" from *Stone Hammer Poems*, © Robert Kroetsch (Lantzville, B.C.: Oolichan Books, 1975). Reprinted by permission.

Sections "a" and "b" from *The Ledger*, © Robert Kroetsch (Ilderton, Ont.: Brick/Nairn, 1975). Reprinted by permission.

MARGARET LAURENCE:

"The Mask of the Bear" from *A Bird in the House* by Margaret Laurence. Used by permission of the Canadian Publishers, McClelland and Stewart, Toronto.

DOROTHY LIVESAY:

"Why We Are Here" from *Ice Age*, © Dorothy Livesay (Victoria: Press Porcépic, 1975). Reprinted by permission.

"Euthanasia" from *Feeling the Worlds*, © Dorothy Livesay (Fredericton: Fiddlehead Books, 1984). Reprinted by permission.

"Improvisation on an Old Theme," "After Hiroshima," "Other," "The Uninvited" and "Threshold" from *Collected Poems: The Two Seasons*, © Dorothy Livesay (Scarborough: McGraw-Hill Ryerson Limited, 1972). Reprinted by permission.

JACK LUDWIG:

"Requiem for Bibul," © 1960 Jack Ludwig, first published in *The Atlantic Monthly*. Reprinted by permission.

BRIAN MacKINNON:

"The Bedside Stories" and "I Told the Circle of Holy Women" from *Fathers and Heroes*, © Brian MacKinnon (Winnipeg: Prairie Publishing Co., 1982). Reprinted by permission.

KENNETH McROBBIE:

"Making It Light" and "Dust Before Rain" from *What Is On Fire Is Happening*, © Kenneth McRobbie (Winnipeg: Four Humours Press, 1975). Reprinted by permission.

ANGELA MEDWID:

"O Pen Let Her," © Angela Medwid, first appeared in *Contemporary Verse 2*, Vol. 9, Nos. 3 & 4 (Winter 1986). Reprinted by permission.

AUDREY POETKER:

"touching home" from *i sing for my dead in german*, © Audrey Poetker (Winnipeg: Turnstone Press, 1986). Reprinted by permission.

SINCLAIR ROSS:

"Cornet at Night" from *The Lamp at Noon* by Sinclair Ross. Used by permission of the Canadian Publishers, McClelland and Stewart, Toronto.

THOMAS SAUNDERS:

"Scrub Oak" and "Cottonwood" from *Beyond the Lakes*, © Thomas Saunders (Winnipeg: Peguis Publishers Limited, 1978). Reprinted by permission.

CAROL SHIELDS:

"Flitting Behavior" from *Various Miracles*, © Carol Shields, 1985. Reprinted by permission of the Author and Stoddart Publishing Co. Limited.

DOUGLAS SMITH:

"The History of Flight" and "Bird Brain" from *Scarecrow*, © Douglas Smith (Winnipeg: Turnstone Press, 1980). Reprinted by permission.

JACQUI SMYTH:

"Delusion," © Jacqui Smyth, first appeared in *Northern Light*, #6. Reprinted by permission.

WAYNE TEFS:

"Mints for Mrs H," © Wayne Tefs, will appear in a forthcoming issue of *The Antigonish Review*. Reprinted by permission.

MYRON TURNER:

"The Crab" from *Rag Doll's Shadow*, © Myron Turner (Erin, Ont.: The Porcupine's Quill, 1979). Reprinted by permission.

"Children" from *Playing the Numbers*, © Myron Turner (Grand Forks, ND: North Dakota Quarterly Press, 1986). Reprinted by permission.

EDWARD UPWARD:

"the shed" from *Pastoral Madness*, © Edward Upward (Winnipeg: Turnstone Press, 1981). Reprinted by permission.

W.D. VALGARDSON:

"The Couch," © W.D. Valgardson, first appeared in *The Saturday Evening Post*. Reprinted by permission.

MIRIAM WADDINGTON:

"Ukrainian Church," "Fortunes," "From a Dead Poet's Book," "The Nineteen Thirties Are Over," "Popular Geography," "Provincial" and "The New Seasons: Light and Dark" from *Collected Poems*, © Miriam Waddington (Don Mills: Oxford University Press Canada, 1986). Reprinted by permission.

ARMIN WIEBE:

"These Troubled Times" from *The Salvation of Yasch Siemens*, © Armin Wiebe (Winnipeg: Turnstone Press, 1984). Reprinted by permission.

ADELE WISEMAN:

Excerpts from *Old Markets, New World*, © Adele Wiseman (Toronto: Macmillan of Canada, 1964). Reprinted by permission.

DALE ZIEROTH:

"Manitoba Poem" and "The Hunters of the Deer" from *Clearing: Poems from a Journey* (Toronto: House of Anansi Press, 1973). Reprinted by permission.

CONTENTS

INTRODUCTION xxi

ARTHUR ADAMSON

Spell of Trees 3

In the House by the Prairie 4

GEORGE AMABILE

Canto 6

Churches 7

Word Games 8

Rain 8

prairie 10

DAVID ARNASON

Sons and Fathers, Fathers and Sons 12

SANDRA BIRDSELL

The Bride Doll 24

KATE BITNEY

Noon And My Sisters 38

I Am Shown The Land 38

DI BRANDT

ruling his shrunken kingdom 41

i wish the sky was still pasted on 42

& i what do i want 42

Diana 43

LOIS BRAUN

The Edge of the Cornfield 46

DENNIS COOLEY
Fielding 53
shapes of frost 56
corvus brachyrhynchos 57
by the red 58
dear valentine 60
day hardens 61
Travelling Back 63
CHESTER DUNCAN
Up and Down in the Depression 65
PATRICK FRIESEN
excerpts from *The Shunning* 71
terrain 75
wings 75
sunday afternoon 76
dream of the black river 78
KEITH LOUISE FULTON
there is no special structure women have 80
KRISTJANA GUNNARS
From Memory I 81
From Memory II 82
From Memory XII 84
Stefán Eyjólfsson XV 85
Jóhann Briem 2, II 87
A Long Production 89
JAN HORNER
A Letter to My Mother 90
MARY HORODYSKI
Housecraft 92
At 7 93

SMARO KAMBOURELI
excerpts from *in the second person:*
Wednesday, December 21, 1980 97
February 6, 1981 97
February 8, 1981 98
Banff/August 5, 1981 99

ROBERT KROETSCH
Syllogisms of Desire 100
Projected Visit 102
excerpt from *The Ledger* 103

MARGARET LAURENCE
The Mask of the Bear 108

DOROTHY LIVESAY
Euthanasia 131
Why We Are Here 132
After Hiroshima 133
Improvisation on an Old Theme 134
The Uninvited 135
Threshold 136
Other 136

JACK LUDWIG
Requiem for Bibul 139

BRIAN MACKINNON
I Told the Circle of Holy Women 153
The Bedside Stories 154

KENNETH MCROBBIE
Making It Light 155
Dust Before Rain 155

ANGELA MEDWID
O Pen Let Her 158

AUDREY POETKER
touching home 162

SINCLAIR ROSS
Cornet at Night 164

THOMAS SAUNDERS
Scrub Oak 183
Cottonwood 184

CAROL SHIELDS
Flitting Behavior 185

DOUGLAS SMITH
The History of Flight 197
Bird Brain 198

JACQUI SMYTH
Delusion 199

WAYNE TEFS
Mints for Mrs H 201

MYRON TURNER
The Crab 208
Children 209

ED UPWARD
the shed 210

W.D. VALGARDSON
The Couch 212

MIRIAM WADDINGTON
Ukrainian Church 230
Fortunes 231
From a Dead Poet's Book 233
The Nineteen Thirties Are Over 234
Popular Geography 236
Provincial 237
The New Seasons: Light and Dark 239

ARMIN WIEBE
These Troubled Times 242

ADELE WISEMAN
excerpts from *Old Markets, New World* 256

DALE ZIEROTH
Manitoba Poem 264
The Hunters of the Deer 265

Introduction

I

In a 1983 review of three regional anthologies, David Jackel outlines in convincing fashion the objections many critics have to such projects:

> The primary problem for most editors compiling a collection of Canadian short stories is this: how to justify its existence. Books that give us the previously scattered stories of a good writer are self-justifying; collections of the "best" stories, or the "best new" stories, of a particular year are justified if the editor is a good judge of literary merit; textbooks rest their claims on the existence of a real or imagined market. Beyond these examples lie the majority of recent collections, which are assembled on stylistic, thematic, or territorial premises, and are occasionally justified by good editorial judgment but more often defended by ingenious special pleading.

This is an intelligent criticism, and I am in at least partial agreement with it. Nevertheless, I intend to do a little special pleading of my own here, for as editor of this "territorial" anthology it is my position that a collection of poems and short stories by Manitoba writers can not only be justified but seen as a valuable addition to our culture. These are brave words—some will say hyperbolic—but the days of the prairie literary inferiority complex are over. Canadian literature consists of more than just what comes out of Toronto and Montreal, and, yes, we too deserve to be heard.

If this sounds aggressive, consider what Canadian literature as a whole has been up against for the past century, and then apply the same lesson to the current imbalance of cultural power in this country. As Margaret Atwood has argued, Canadians have waged a long struggle on many fronts, but particularly the literary one, against the notion that "'there' is always more important than 'here' or that 'here' is just another, inferior, version of 'there'." This perception has changed radically over the past twenty years, the Booker nominations for Atwood's and Davies's work being the most obvious symbol of that shift. There are wheels within wheels, however, and it is difficult to avoid the impression, especially in the East, that everything important is produced in our larger cultural centres. As Dennis Cooley has said:

> If Canadians as a whole have suffered from the notion that intelligence exists or can be tested only out there, somewhere (in France or England or the U.S.), Canadians have applied those kinds of notions within their own country. Every cosmopolite knows, or should know, that our national genius, by one of those extraordinary miracles of history, has chosen to reside within the city limits of Toronto. Given all the other circumstances which already meant nobody on the Prairies could have much hope of becoming a legitimate poet, this ingrained prejudice virtually guaranteed such things wouldn't happen.

Western writers, in other words, now find themselves in more or less the same position that Canadian writers did in an earlier time: striving to be heard over much louder voices.

II

An interesting historical parallel can be drawn between this striving of regional writers for equality and the "cosmopolitan vs. national" debates of A.J.M. Smith and John Sutherland in the 1940s. Smith insisted that Canadians adopt a cosmopolitan approach to literature or, as he put it, the "entering into the universal, civilizing culture of ideas," while Sutherland advocated a national perspective, maintaining that Canadian literature would come of age when it "has stopped being a parasite on other literatures and has had the courage to decide its own problems in its own way." Smith was chiefly reacting against the so-called Maple Leaf School of "boosters" who operated under the aegis of the Canadian Authors' Association, and he was right to do so. The prejudice persists, however, only now on a regional level, that for prairie writers to be concerned with fashioning a literature out of their own place and time and in their own voices is to be insular and unsophisticated.

Of course, universality and "localism" have never been antonyms, as the highly localized fictions of Joyce, Faulkner and Marquez demonstrate. Louis Dudek puts it this way: "Smith...sees universality in terms of the current turning to world events; whereas I see it in terms of observed human experience, local experience, presented in universal terms. This is the great issue, 'a local pride' (Williams and Souster) or intellectual internationalism." Prairie writers, like Dudek, seem eager to adopt this "middle ground" between obsequious servility to "the great tradition" and chauvinist boosterism. Robert Kroetsch has said that "only when we decreate ourselves and the inauthentic borrowings from other cultures which we have borrowed with colonial tenacity, will authentic self-definition be possible." At the same time, his own writing has been heavily influenced by a variety of foreign models, notably the South American "magic realists." Perhaps the best expression of this dialectic is provided in Kroetsch's dictum (if it's possible for a post-modernist to provide dictums) that "To lose the tradition is fatal, but to surrender to it is fatal."

The term "local pride" crops up again in an interview with the same writer. When asked how he can square the idea that foreign models should be avoided with the admission that William Carlos Williams is one of his main sources of inspiration, Kroetsch replies,

"You don't imitate, you emulate.... You take the lesson, not the actual poem. Look at the beginning of 'Paterson' with those three words, 'a local pride'. A local pride is where you've got to begin from, and we didn't even have a local pride. Because all the models were telling us we didn't even exist."

The shock of discovering that one not only exists but that one's place and people are worthy of literature is expressed in the following excerpt from a conversation with Margaret Laurence:

> I remember—I must have been in my late teens, I suppose—when I read Sinclair Ross' novel, *As For Me and My House*, which was about a minister in a small prairie town; it hit me with tremendous force, because I realized for the first time that people could really write about my background.... You know, I read Kipling, and what the hell did Kipling have to do with where I was living? And that isn't to say that we shouldn't read widely, but it is a good thing to be able to read, as a child, something that belongs to you, belongs to your people.

Both writers are eager, then, to strike a balance between regionalism and internationalism. Interestingly enough, it is a balance reflected in their lives: Laurence, the native Manitoban who decided to leave but, like Joyce, set the majority of her fiction in the place of her birth; Kroetsch, the prairie boy from Heisler, who lit out for the U.S. but eventually adopted Manitoba as his home. Both insist on assimilating the lessons foreign writers provide, while throwing off or "uninventing" the barriers of false voice and "fit subjects" which would impede our own story.

III

What is that story and how is it told? A complete answer to that question is beyond the scope of this introduction, but the variety of themes and forms collected here will doubtless come as a surprise to those accustomed to thinking of prairie literature as one-dimensional, the last bastion of gritty naturalism. According to that view, prairie literature is chiefly composed of stories featuring settlers and farmers fighting insurmountable odds, only to be finally subdued by an implacable, hostile Nature. As Warren Tallman once elegantly put it, the conventional prairie images of dust, grain elevators and the wind "speak of a tragedy in which the desire to prevail that drives self on its strange journeys toward fulfillment is brought to an impasse on northern fields of a continent which has remained profoundly indifferent to its inhabitant, transplanted European man." Laurence Ricou summarizes this view in a more straightforward fashion: "Man on the prairie...is defined especially by two things: exposure, and an awareness of the surrounding emptiness.... Such exposure, compounded by the rigours of a northern climate, inevitably prompts the theme of man's aloneness in a hostile, or at the least indifferent, universe."

No one can deny that these positions accurately describe much of the fiction produced in Manitoba over the past sixty years. The names of Ross, Grove and Ostenso spring to mind. It is equally undeniable, however, that many writers in this province have grown impatient with the old stereotypes and approach Nature in either an entirely different way or not at all. Continuing urbanization, on the social level, and the desire to experiment with new forms, on the literary level, have resulted in a broadening of perceptions.

The great prairie realists of the '20s and '30s were also responding to the need for fresh perceptions, their stark realism a reaction to the sanitized, transplanted romanticism of their predecessors; but, as T.E. Hulme has illustrated in reference to a very different literature, conventions have a habit of ossifying. For the new prairie writers, realism is nothing more than that: a convention—not a window to truth—and one which needs to be balanced by fabulation, humour and, above all, the free rein of the imagination. Listen to some Manitoba writers on this subject:

David Arnason: Again, what I want to escape from are the traditional patterns of the mimetic storyteller who tells the same thing. It's tough enough coming from the prairies where everybody who picks up the book assumes that a young man growing up in a bitter windswept prairie town will earn his manhood by facing a railway train on a trestle. It's just about time the country grew out of those assumptions.

Wayne Tefs: [We are] finding new ways to begin.... Sweeping away something oppressive about the naturalistic view of things, and giving a wider sweep to the powers and potentials of the human intelligence. Each opening that risks such imaginative scope takes the prairie novel one step further away from the ironic vision of the realistic landscape novel toward a more triumphant human perspective—of men and women celebrating life and giving it human energy and shape.

Robert Kroetsch: What has come to interest me right now is what I suppose you can call the dream of origins. Obviously in the prairies, the small town and the farm are not merely places, they are remembered places. When they were the actuality of our lives, we had realistic fiction, and we had almost no poetry at all. Now in this dream condition, as dream-time fuses into the kind of narrative we call myth, we change the nature of the novel. And we start, with a new and terrible energy, to write the poems of the imagined real place.

Douglas Smith: If we are reading a poem about a grain elevator, why should we find out at the end what we already know: that there is flax or wheat inside? Why can't a winged condor burst through the roof?

Critics such as Eli Mandel and Dick Harrison have also grown weary with the old formulations. Mandel takes Edward McCourt to task for emphasizing "accuracy" in prairie realism, suggesting that "'accurate description' really means the imitation of certain easy clichés and stereotypes about landscape and environment." At the same time he points to a number of features of prairie literature—

the grotesque, the tall tale, the emphasis on children—which tend to be forgotten in our haste to make everything conform to the strictures of naturalism. Harrison turns the tables on those who blame the prairie environment for impeding the production of great literature: "...I am insisting that the plight of the imagination is to be blamed not so much on the environment as on a long cultural tradition of inadequate response to it...." He also insists that the hegemony of the "tragic" view of prairie life has been largely the result of critical and academic myopia—promoting one group of writers, however brilliant, and one world-view at the expense of others. As Roland Barthes has noted, "Literature is what gets taught."

The reader of this anthology, then, will find more than gritty realism and tales of despair. Perhaps, in the words of Wayne Tefs, it will be possible to discover "men and women celebrating life and giving it human energy and shape."

IV

Deciding who qualifies as a Manitoba writer has been, for the most part, an easy task. The great majority of the writers collected here have lived and worked in the province for all or almost all their lives. When it came to the "special cases," I decided to err on the side of inclusiveness. Some writers, Robert Kroetsch for example, while not born in the province, have been here for a substantial period of time and produced a sizeable body of work while residing in Manitoba. Although I am not completely convinced one should limit the selections to what a writer has produced while actually living in the province, I have, almost always, done so. Kroetsch is represented here, then, not as a novelist but as a poet, the majority of his poetic production having taken place over the past decade. In the case of Miriam Waddington, I have decided to include poems which, in the main, make specific reference to her earlier life in Manitoba.

Finally, it may seem presumptuous to claim Dorothy Livesay as a Manitoba poet, yet she is one, in addition to being a Vancouver poet, a Montreal poet and a world poet; and I'm not just referring to the fact that she spent her formative years here, documented so engagingly in *A Winnipeg Childhood*, and several of her later ones, writing the extraordinary poems of *Ice Age* and editing *CVII*. She is the perfect example of the kind of writer Eli Mandel refers to in his recent essay, "Writing West: On the Road to Wood Mountain." The western writer is:

> not necessarily the one who is in the west, or who stays here, but the one who returns, who moves, who points in this direction.... [It] is not place but attitude, state of mind that defines the western writer—and that state of mind...has a good deal to do with a tension between place and culture, a doubleness or duplicity, that makes the writer a man not so much in place, as out of place and so one endlessly trying to get back, to find his way home, to return, to write himself into existence, writing west.

If one can ignore the masculine pronouns, this passage sounds remarkably similar to what Livesay herself wrote about a trip across Canada after years in Africa:

> To get the feel of my own country again I drove with my son Peter from Vancouver to my birthplace, Winnipeg.... By the time we reached Winnipeg I was steeped in sensations, so reminiscent of my childhood, of black soil sliding into open sky. Although I had originally hoped to write an objective documentary—a "cross-country checkup" from the Pacific to the Atlantic—I ended abruptly and subjectively in Winnipeg. My beginnings were there. I knew: Manitoba, pivotal, facing east and west, could be the right place for an ending.

V

Most of the other writers represented here have written almost all their work in the past twenty-five years. Given the choice between putting together an anthology dominated by the old or the new, I have chosen the latter. Would that the book could be twice the size and had room for Roy, Ostenso, Grove, Marlyn and Hiebert; would that it could be thrice the size and had room for a host of fine young Manitoba writers who deserve a wider audience. I have not been able to resist including a Ross story, but it is one that has perhaps had less exposure than his others and which shows us another side of this splendid writer.

In choosing the materials, I have tried not to work from a preconceived notion of what such an anthology ought to contain, at least in the terms dictated by past criticism. Granted, the encounter with an unforgiving land is reflected in several pieces, and much of the fiction is either explicitly set in the province or reflects what Kroetsch has called "a hovering care for place." Many other selections, however, crystallize parts of the human experience in Manitoba which have not been accorded a place in the rigid confines of our critical thinking.

Finally, although I have tried hard to strike ethnic, gender-based, regional, thematic and formal balances, my most important criterion has been something quite simple: everything collected here gives me pleasure. My fervent hope is that this book can provide the same gift for all its readers.

Mark Duncan

BIBLIOGRAPHY

The quotations in the introduction are taken from the following sources. Those interested in additional critical materials on Manitoba and Prairie literature should consult the excellent bibliography in Birk Sproxton's *Trace: Prairie Writers on Writing*.

Jackel, David. "Particulars." *Canadian Literature* 96 (Spring, 1983), 151-153.

Atwood, Margaret. *Survival*. Toronto: Anansi, 1972.

Cooley, Dennis (ed). *RePlacing*. Downsview: ECW Press, 1980.

Smith, A.J.M. Introduction to *The Book of Canadian Poetry*. Chicago: University of Chicago Press, 1943.

Sutherland, John. "Literary Colonialism." *First Statement*, Vol. 2, no. 4 (1944).

Dudek, Louis. "Dirty Linen?" *Canadian Literature* 40 (Spring, 1969), 99-100.

Lecker, Robert. *Robert Kroetsch*. Boston: Twayne Publishers, 1986.

Kroetsch, Robert. Essays. An issue of *Open Letter*, Fifth Series, No. 4 (Spring, 1983).

Cooley, Dennis and Enright, Robert. "Uncovering our Dream-World: An Interview with Robert Kroetsch." *Arts Manitoba* Vol. 1, No. 1 (January/February, 1977), 32-39.

Kroetsch, Robert (ed). *Creation*. Toronto, Chicago: New Press, 1970.

Tallman, Warren. "Wolf in the Snow," Parts One and Two. *Canadian Literature* 5 and 6 (1960), 7-20 and 41-48.

Ricou, Laurence. *Vertical Man/Horizontal World*. Vancouver: University of British Columbia Press, 1973.

Sproxton, Birk. *Trace*. Winnipeg: Turnstone Press, 1986.

Smith, Douglas. Introduction to *Northern Light* No. 6 (Summer, 1981).

Mandel, Eli. "Images of Prairie Man." *Another Time*. Erin: Press Porcépic, 1977.

Harrison, Dick. *Unnamed Country*. Edmonton: University of Alberta Press, 1977.

Livesay, Dorothy. *The Documentaries*. Toronto: Ryerson Press, 1968.

SECTION LINES:
A MANITOBA ANTHOLOGY

ARTHUR ADAMSON

Spell of Trees

for Joyce

to the spell of trees
their gesture and speech
to them in fiery green or to
them quilted   numb   or in consort of
the wind and where
in magical motion birds
resort   or in winter   leafless   dark
and stark   I turn and still seek all
the gathered connivings
of quiet and storm   fit
season's convenings

                                        they
brittle in sweep of splintered rake
of january sun   startle and
dance in stillness   fire
particles strewn from
crust and frost   stiff
conjugal stance   then
stunned in the turn
of an inching sun   bland
stars incite sudden
flame-broken leaves

in their stasis and stir
I   wintered man
then summered   sing

In the House by the Prairie

in the house surrounded by trees
pinned by noon's riddle of light
genial ghosts have taken the air
leaving smells of linoleum   stale wood
old chairs   dusty panes   fast spiders
a harbour of shadow and beyond
the blaze of meadow   weight
of the sun and the meadow lark's song

the summer smells pressed with heat
thicken in drifts through the leaves
as slow afternoon blunts our near
awareness of hours   inner green
birdsong and silence   on the floor
the scrub oak litters the worn
rug in sour patches of pale
light and the red plush stands fire

when I came out of the shower
in the recessed house all my wet
skin flashed a blur in the glass
door   there my destitute self
took green clothing   wild weed and bush
sank into my bone   I was made
a summer man like the sun
and in that guise we made love

the green man rose to the room
above the house smells and summer
glaze and the light failed and frogs
sang and the oriole's song died
a fired moth turned to ash
in green shadow   sun froze on the wall
in blotchy oblongs of pale light
the green man sank to his flesh

the air dimmed and the wind died
there was far thunder   in the light's shift
lightning winked the day's fall

GEORGE AMABILE

Canto

for Pablo Neruda

Musician of stern autumns and whispering steel
maestro of the mind's muscle
your violent flowers & delicate storms invade us
like the miracles of an affectionate technology

Sure
even in darkness
you walk along a desolate coast
your ancient head silvered by moonlight
and battered by invisible capes of the wind

You are crooning to the surrounding night
in a clean voice full of surprises
the shy loves of weeds and lichen
boots tomatoes and salt

On the far shore
men still shovel coal & dusty ore in the red ghost-light of the mills
Their sweat shines like the oil of your poems
women spread their wrinkled wash over shrubs in the early sun
They are serene, and heavy with music
and the children run barefoot through the shadows of century plants
Their laughter cracks open and blossoms in the wind

Churches

1

There are no stars.
Down the street
a wizard's hat of dusty light
fills with children.

2

I lean against an iron fence
on which the paint has broken out in buds
of rust. In there
morning glories
have sucked their blue trumpets
into puckered mouths and tight little fists
under a sprinkling of coal dust.

3

Dressed in black
these crones mumble and nod
under a wooden crucifixion
as though they had taken leave
of their lives
dredging up mystery
with gnarled incantations
waiting for the Eternity express.

Candles burn in red glass.
There's a cough
that echoes
as shadows jostle the vaulted windows
in which the lives of saints
(and villains)
are stacked like a card house.

Word Games

I've learned this much
at least: process
is not a system.

When we use the word
to describe cheese
or as a verb (please

process this application)
we are being very sly
and very stupid.

As though we could con
the whole damn universe
into being what we'd like

it to be: a big
machine we know
how to use as a weapon.

Rain

Miracles occur
If you care to call those spasmodic
Tricks of radiance miracles
— Sylvia Plath

Down the street
a sunday of empty parks

Clouds assemble
like the grey stones in a prison wall
and the river's blown ripple patterns
grow still
as a crowd before a hanging

I've walked all day
through puddles & dirty windows
backed by the sky's thickening light

When it starts
it's cold
& drowsy as hemlock
I find a doorway's glass box
To the right
to the left
clocks display
their blank numbered faces
combed by spidery arms
behind my face
which hangs in the glass
balanced
between this universe of wheels   whirrs   insect speech
and a town wiped out by rain

Inklings breathe
at the back of my mind
like the unshelled bodies of snails
But mouselight and hypnosis
precipitate
long spattering bursts

The overcast breaks up like rotten ice
and wherever sunlight lights the bouncing rain
on the sleek tar
on the rinsed roofs and hoods and bumpers of cars
even on flat water
it surprises thousands
of horned creatures the color of glass
whose looked through lives become visible
whenever they have something to dance about

prairie

a light word
filled with wistful spokes
of sun through the overcast at dusk
or smoke totems bent at the top
wisping away into beige emulsions

an earth word
a moist darkness turning
stones and roots
fossils and tiny lives
up to the sun

a watery word
mirage and heat lightning
steadied by pewter barns
where whole towns float in a lilting haze
and rumors of rain rise from the rapeseed lakes

a flame shaped word
a ragged mane blowing
for miles across dry grass
lighting the night like fired breath
out of the old testament

a word with air
in its belly that howls
for hours or days and dries
the memory of soft conversation
to wheatdust under the tongue

like the distance we've come
to stand here in the sky at the top of the world

DAVID ARNASON

Sons and Fathers, Fathers and Sons

There is something about fathers and sons that could do with an explanation a little less mechanical than Freud's. Anybody who is both a father and a son will know what I mean. It's a devious business, this sending your genes out into the world in a body over which you no longer have control. It calls for extreme measures, and any relationship between a father and a son is organized around extremes. Nothing is unfair.

Let me begin. I was born in a real, honest-to-goodness tar-paper shack. In that sense, my proletarian credentials are impeccable. To be perfectly honest, I was actually born in a quite up-to-date hospital, attended by a doctor who, though inclined to forgetfulness, nevertheless had all his papers. I went directly from the hospital to the shack, where I spent the next three months until my father completed the house he was building. You see, I'm trying to be honest with you, though I'm not sure that's always the best policy. That shack, however little time I spent in it, is a metaphor of my beginnings.

My son, on the other hand, was born, at least relatively, into the lap of luxury. He moved directly into a basement suite. It was a natural childbirth, not that it was intended to be. He merely came too fast for the doctor to use any of the arcane methods modern doctors prefer. He was already in this world complaining about it before they even got his mother into the delivery room. He was saved the indignity that I faced, hauled into the world by a pair of forceps, my head squeezed so out of shape that in baby pictures I look vaguely hydrocephalic.

I was by all accounts a clumsy child. I never learned how to crawl, and though I learned to walk relatively early, my first use of this newly discovered talent was to hurl myself down the basement stairs, landing fortunately on the dog, a large yellow mongrel named Bruno. Bruno, for his services in saving my infant neck, demanded his pound of flesh. He bit me in the leg, leaving me with a fear of dogs that is in no way diminished today.

My father was what in those days was called a Jack-of-All-Trades, and my clumsiness troubled him sorely. He had been a champion hockey player and a champion baseball player. It was clear to him by the time I was a year old that I was not going to be a champion anything. Later, when I went to university, I proved him wrong by becoming a champion ping-pong player, a sport which he had always loathed for its effeminacy. He congratulated me, but his congratulations came from a constricted throat and a puckered mouth.

My son, as you've probably guessed by now, is a first-rate athlete. He is the one chosen first for all teams. He plays games with a kind of easy abandon that makes difficult manoeuvres look like simple acts of nature. He has also a disquieting interest in the mechanical and the scientific, just the right qualifications for a Jack-of-All-Trades. He takes difficult things apart, things like clocks and cameras, and he puts them back together so that they continue to function. I remember my father's disgust at my own lack of coordination, the thumbs struck by hammers or caught in car doors, the machinery put hopelessly out of adjustment by my ministrations. The workings of hydraulic brakes or power steering systems remain profoundly mysterious to me, however often my father explained that only a fool could fail to see at first glance how they function.

Not that my father was really much better coordinated than I am. He bent nails. His chisel slipped, and there was always something slightly askew in the kitchen cupboards he made. He hit fairly well-placed grounders that would never have got him to first base in a slightly better league, but were enough to make him a star in the leagues he played in. He did everything with a dogged intensity that carried his world before him. In me, he was looking for grace, but all he got was his own slight case of butterfingers without the will to overcome it.

He envies me my son who is everything he wanted me to be, everything he wanted to be himself. My son who can even sing in tune. I come from a family of tone-deaf bellowers. People often ask us what we are trying to say when we are in full song, which is even worse than being accused of being a bad singer. They can't even tell that we're trying to sing. We all own pianos and guitars and drawers full of mouth organs that none of us can play.

What is worst for my father is the knowledge that none of my son's graceful genes come from him. My son is tall and lithe, with wide shoulders and narrow hips, like the men of my wife's family, like the women of my wife's family for that. My father and his four brothers are middle-sized men with chests like barrels and short, thick, powerful legs. The women out of that mould make spectacular teenage girls, but go to fat early. My wife's family, on the other hand, call to mind greyhounds or thoroughbred horses. Thankfully, they are lazy and shiftless, as my father succinctly puts it, or else they would be unbearable.

I bear, unfortunately, a stunning resemblance to my father. At forty-five, I'm grey and balding, five-foot eight and barrel-chested. I'm a successful psychiatrist, though I look as if I should be moving mattresses, and in fact, whenever I dare to dress casually, I am mistaken for janitors and repairmen. I've tried wearing a large gold ring with diamonds in it to prevent this, but it doesn't help.

Oddly, it bothers my son that he bears no resemblance to me. He likes it when lying aunts point out some mysterious similarity in our eyes or our jawbones. There is none. All he has inherited from me is a kind of desperate insecurity and bottomless desire for praise, which I got from my father, and he, I suppose, got from his, and so on back to some frightened paleolithic cave-son stalking a mammoth, in order to satisfy the unspoken demands of his cave-father.

How do you praise a son to whom everything is easy? He is always winning something. Our house is littered with trophies, his jacket is heavy with crests. He reports all his successes, or he used to report them until he discovered they made me uncomfortable. Now he hides them, and the neighbours tell me. It is not even possible to praise his effort, because he seems to put in no effort, though of course that can't be true. I suspect that I am only able to accept as honest effort those attempts that lead you to tears of frustration.

And that, of course, brings me to our moose hunt. Don't worry, no moose will die in this story. Not a shot will be fired in anger. The entire debacle was my own fault, and though I didn't admit it then, I admit it now. The flaw was reminiscence. My father used to take me hunting when I was young, and in the cold light of day I can remember how painful those trips were: hours of huddled crouching in marshes or in frozen bushes, shivering and wet, hoping that nothing living would stray into my range so that I would have to shoot at it. Miles of walking through deep and nearly impenetrable bush carrying heavy packs full of supplies. Yet, one evening, telling my son about my youth, I seemed only to be able to remember sitting around campfires late at night, the taste of bacon and eggs and coffee cooked over an open fire, sunrise over a lake so clear it was a perfect mirror. When my son, taken in by my poetic raptures, suggested that we go hunting moose, I was as excited as he was. We sat up late making our plans.

By the next morning I had come to my senses, though not quickly enough to avoid some sort of gesture at a hunting trip. I decided to go out to Anderson Point. There had been moose there when I was young, and it had the added advantage of being thoroughly in the wilderness and yet accessible by boat, so there would be no need to carry equipment or to slug through marshes. There was an old abandoned fishing camp that would allow a roof over our heads in case of rain. I was absolutely certain of bad weather.

I tried my best to conceal the trip from my father. When he heard about it via the women, he hinted broadly that he should be invited. I resisted, and when he was forced finally to ask if he could come, I refused, explaining that the trip was being undertaken to allow me some private moments with my son, and pointing out to my father that his seventy years would not be helpful in case of trouble. He had given up hunting himself some ten years ago, and I suggested that his retirement should not be interrupted. He in turn pointed out his greater experience, his knack at fixing outboard motors that broke down, his superior knowledge of the shoals and reefs that surrounded Anderson Point. I referred him to his recent electrocardiogram which hinted at a heart murmur, and refused to take responsibility for his demise. That left us at a standoff, and though over the next few weeks he continued to fish for an invitation, he did not press the point.

On September 22, my son Greg and I launched the eighteen-foot fibreglass boat I had rented for the occasion into the chilly waters of Washow Creek. The sixty-five-horse Mercury outboard started as smoothly as a Cadillac and the little ten-horse spare I had brought along out of my general mistrust of machinery lay comfortably in the bow. We had enough equipment and supplies to last for a month, though we only intended to be gone for three days. All my life I've been overprepared, a backup ready for any contingency.

We left at noon on a bright sunny day with a slight breeze from the north. I wound my way through the gentle curves of the creek while my son practised making moose calls with a tin can and a piece of string that he drew through the bottom. He'd read about making moose calls in some hunting magazine and, of course, his worked perfectly. It sounded much more authentic than the actual calls of moose on the tape recorder I had brought along.

When we came out of the creek into Blind Bay, the breeze had risen, and the water was getting choppy. By the time we'd crossed the four miles of the bay out into the lake itself, there were rolling swells. And by the time we reached Crow Duck Creek, whitecaps were tossing the tiny canoe that hurried out to intercept us. When we pulled my father on board, he was soaked to the skin and the canoe was half filled with water.

"I didn't decide to come until the last minute," he told us. "Good thing I didn't miss you."

"Yes," I told him, not without a little sarcasm, "that was certainly a good thing. You might have drowned or had a heart attack."

My son, on the other hand, was delighted. He pulled the canoe across the boat and strapped it on, welcoming his grandfather with unrestrained pleasure. He made the old man take off his clothes and offered him some of his own. Standing there in the boat, naked and shivering, my father looked like a figure of the damned out of a Jehovah's Witnesses' handout, but a moment later, clothed in my son's jeans and a rugby shirt, he looked almost maliciously jaunty. The only item of his own apparel that he kept was his old Minerva Gophers baseball cap that he had been threatening for years to give to the town museum. The museum had been less keen on that artifact than my father was, and so it had remained in his possession.

My father proved his necessity by pointing out hidden shoals and disguised rocks. I had no way of knowing whether these were real or imaginary, but I avoided them anyway. As a result, we arrived a couple of hours later than I had expected, and it was dark when we reached Anderson Point. I, frankly, could see nothing, but my father claimed he could tell where we were by the sound of the breakers, and my son actually said he could see a low line of buildings against the uniformly black shore. I followed their directions, and the boat crunched onto gravel right at the fishing camp.

We landed, walked the boat around a small point of land to a pier my father remembered and which was miraculously still there after twenty-five years of abandonment. We emptied the boat, dragged my overload of supplies into what had once been the main bunkhouse, and spread out our sleeping bags on the floor. My father brought out a mickey of rye, which seemed to be the only supplies he had brought, and we each had a throat-scalding swallow. My father and my son were both eager to talk, my father to conjure the death of ancient moose, my son to predict the downfall of future moose. I exerted authority both ways, turned out the flashlight, and insisted on silence.

During the night, I awoke briefly to the patter of rain and the sound of waves crashing on the shore. It was a lulling sound, and I was only briefly apprehensive. When I awoke to the grey light of a feeble dawn, the sleeping bags on either side of me were empty. I clambered into my chilly clothes and went outside. The whitecaps on the lake made it clear that we would be going nowhere in the boat that day. My father was huddled over a small fire, a frying pan in his hands and a coffee pot balanced on a stick.

"Breakfast in ten minutes," he called, as cheerfully and matter-of-factly as if he had a right to be there.

I muttered an okay and went in search of my son. I found him in a filletting shed, studying the graffiti on the walls as if they were Egyptian hieroglyphs.

"Look at this," he said. "June fifteenth, 1947." The wonder in his voice made that date sound inconceivably ancient. "It says J.T. loves M.P. I wonder who they could be?"

J.T. was Jimmy Tomlinson. His father had run this camp, and Jimmy, a classmate of mine, had left school a month early each year to go out here, because his mother was the cook. M.P. would have been Marlene Perkins, my son's mother and my wife. This evidence of an almost prehistoric passion stirred me strangely. Jimmy would have been nine years old at the time of this declaration. I wondered whether his love might have been reciprocated. Marlene was a grade behind us and, frankly, I had been only marginally aware of her existence until I had returned from university one summer, found her working in a drugstore and married her. I knew she had had other lovers, of whom I was retrospectively jealous, but I hadn't known my emotions could go so far back in time.

"I don't know," I told my son. "A lot of fishermen worked here. It could be almost anyone." Jimmy Tomlinson was now an alcoholic, sunk so deep in dissipation that there was little hope for recovery. Still, he was one more scaler of my castle, one more ghost to brood about in the irrational moments just before sleep. "Come on," I said, "Grandpa's got breakfast ready."

The breakfast was delicious, marred only by my father's habit of breaking the yolks of eggs when he cooked them. It was an old family feud, and I stood firmly with my mother on the issue. The yolks of eggs should not be broken. My son, who had never eaten camp-fire cooking, pronounced the meal the best he had ever tasted.

Our plan had been to raid some of the small islands around Anderson Point: Fox Island, Goose Island, Little Punk Island. Moose will swim for miles in the mating season, and there was a very good chance that, with little effort, we might find our quarry. My father explained that the canoe would come in handy because moose liked to feed in the mouths of the dozen small creeks just around the point. I put a damper on the plans by announcing that the weather made it impossible. We would wait until it calmed down. If the waves were smaller in the afternoon, we might try then. My son, who was eager and knew nothing of water, found me unconvincing. My father, who knew better, but who also knew that my conservatism would prevail, argued there was no danger. We stayed.

After that, conversation died. My son took a compass and announced he was going to go into the bush to find birch bark to make more moose calls. The Indians, he explained, always made moose calls out of birch bark. My father, who, since his retirement, had got out of the habit of early rising, announced he was going back to bed. I cautioned my son against the dangers of getting lost in the bush, but having squelched one set of plans, I couldn't garner enough moral force to stop another, and he disappeared into the yellowing bush.

Left alone, I went in search of further evidence of my wife's ghostly presence in the camp. I found it carved in the walls of the slumping outhouse. J.T. loves M.P. June, 1951. It argued a persistent attraction, but left Jimmy at thirteen, not yet old enough to be considered a danger. There had been four Tomlinson boys, all of whom I had considered sullen and introspective. Here on the walls, however, was astonishing evidence of their capacity for love. They had linked their initials with most of the alphabetic possibilities, making that lonely outhouse a monument to passion.

They had also been great makers of birthday cards for their mother. These were posted in the kitchen, and I was examining them for some consistent image when my son returned, interrupting my archeological speculation.

"I got lost," he said, almost proudly. "I checked the compass and it said I was going north. I checked it again about thirty seconds later and it said I was going south."

"You got turned around," I told him. "It's easy to do."

"I didn't believe the compass," he said. "I knew I couldn't have turned around in that short a time. So, since we're on a point, I figured if I went at right angles to the north-south line, I'd have to hit the lake, and I did, and I'm here."

A small thrill of horror ran down my spine. In the line of sons, unfortunately, I have no backups, no second chances. Anderson Point is quite large enough and quite wild enough for one to be lost and not be found. I determined then that my son would not leave my sight again during the trip.

By mid-afternoon, the clouds had cleared. The whitecaps had turned into large rolling swells, and the sun, though it gave no warmth, made everything look bright and clean. We decided to go over to Fox Island, a trip of about three miles. The motor started with a sweet purr, though I turned the key convinced that it could never start. We idled slowly, because I was taking no chances with the swells, which seemed a lot larger as soon as we got around the point. Fox Island loomed ahead, a gigantic rock with sheer cliffs on the face. Around the other side, I knew, there was a gentle sloping shore, but we were making for another abandoned fish camp on the face side. There, a floating dock took you to a set of stairs carved into the cliff, and near the top was a filletting shed set into a niche so that it seemed a part of the cliff face itself. I remembered the view from there as spectacular, and it seemed the kind of reminiscence I might share with my son, recollecting it in twenty years for some future grandson.

The landing was uneventful. We tied up the boat and made our way up the stairs to the filletting shed. My son and I went into the shed to look at the view, and my father continued up the stairs to the top. The view was magnificent. We could see across Anderson Point to Washow Bay on the far side and pick out four or five other small islands. I heard a strange scuffling noise, as if someone were walking on the roof, then a thump, and suddenly my father appeared before us, looking in the window from outside. He seemed to hover a second, as if he had something he wanted to say, and then he was gone with a splash into the water below. I froze with horror, but my son was out the door in a second. I followed, and the last thing I saw was the bottom of his shoes as he dived forty feet down to the lake below.

By the time I made my way down to the bottom of the cliff, my son had dragged his grandfather up onto the floating dock and was administering mouth-to-mouth resuscitation. The old man came to, choking and spluttering and cursing, as much horrified by the touch of male lips on his, I suspect, as by his near encounter with death. I was in a rage, wanting someone to blame besides myself, and knowing there was no one. I ordered them both into the boat and started the motor. It churned into life and I headed back to Anderson Point a lot faster than I knew I should. About a hundred yards from the dock, the motor coughed and stopped. I turned the key and heard a whining hum.

Details bore me, and they'd bore you too. I could describe my soaking father, hardly out of death's kingdom and already tinkering with the motor, my modest heroic son, eager to please, helping him. I'm not going to describe that, nor am I going to describe my churlish self, bad-tempered and clumsy, getting in the way, giving orders that had no possibility of being carried out. All I can tell you is that something happened in the water, some conjunction between the two that excluded me. They looked at each other like new lovers, they spoke to each other with shy politeness, they sidestepped me like you might sidestep an aggressive puppy.

And so it went for the rest of the trip. They fixed the motor. Back at camp, they prepared supper and talked eagerly of the next day's hunt. They ignored my pleas for darkness and sat up until late, polishing off the now sacramental mickey of rye whiskey. The next day, the two of them took the canoe and hunted in the creek mouths, my decision to keep my son in sight overridden by their desire. I pleaded a headache and stayed at the camp, reconstructing the history of the Tomlinson family, *père, mère* and *fils.* I grew to like them for their unreserved ability to carve their feelings into trees and walls. In a moment of inspiration I went back to the outhouse, obliterated Jimmy Tomlinson's initials from the heart that also contained my wife, and replaced them with my own. A petty act, you say, a futile attempt to change history which can't be changed? We'll see.

By the time I'd prepared supper my heart was brimful of love for both my father and my son. I had determined that I would wrest forgiveness from them if I had to wrestle them to the ground to get it. Even when darkness came and they had still not returned I was confident. Even after I had launched the boat, rounded the point and come on the empty floating canoe, I felt no despair. I willed them onto land, chose Little Grindstone Point a mile away as the spot I would find them, waving from the shore. I went directly there, swept the shore with my powerful flashlight, and picked them out standing on the rocky beach where they had to be. I leaped from the boat before it even grounded on the shore, churned my way through the splashing waves and seized them both in a bearhug. We swirled, the three of us in a little dance of joy and love.

I refused all explanations and apologies, refused to explain how I knew where they were until we had made our way back to camp and we had finished the meal I had prepared. Then I opened the bottle of Scotch I had brought and poured us each a large ceremonial drink. I began with my version of events, a carefully embroidered version in which heroism and comic humiliation played a large part. Then my father, taking his cue, added another layer to the evolving myth. My son wound our versions together and opened new possibilities. We sat around that fire until dawn, telling and retelling what had happened, until we had a single version that belonged to us all, carved in the wordless night. To my surprise, I came out at the centre, not at the margins as I had thought I would. There was no need to forgive or ask forgiveness. The story did that for us all.

Just one postscript. The trip back was uneventful, except that the motor refused to start again, and this time we had to use the backup ten-horse. As we were driving back along the old highway, a gigantic moose stepped out of the bush and stood on the road watching us, gleaming black as if it were wet. After a brief flurry of excitement as we reached for guns, we decided that the hunt had been too much of a success to ruin it now by killing a moose. And when I got home and asked my wife about Jimmy Tomlinson, she couldn't even remember who he was.

SANDRA BIRDSELL

The Bride Doll

"A pretty wedding was solemnized," Virginia Colpitts read. "Pink and white peonies and blue delphinium in white baskets were placed on the altar and satin bows designated pews reserved for the guests."

Virginia and I lay out on a blanket in her back yard. We had always lived on the same street. First she had lived at the top of the street in an unpainted, unsteady house which had not survived the last flooding of the river, and then at the bottom of the street, in a bright new bungalow.

We lay in the shadow of a red barn, seeking shelter from the hot dry wind, and read accounts of weddings, placing ourselves inside the church as honoured guests. I was smitten by the descriptions of veils, seed pearls and lily-point sleeves. I imagined satin to be as iridescent as moths' wings, shiny and silvery. I gleaned notices of weddings from the columns in the *Agassiz Herald* and then on Saturdays, Virginia and I waited outside to catch a glimpse of the newly married couple as they came from the church, looking over-starched with self-consciousness. Where once the couple had been as close as Siamese twins, they stood apart, awkward in their new state. I imagined doves fluttering above their heads.

Even though I had been taught not to pray for tangible things as that was a mark of selfishness (a waste of God's valuable time when one considered the numberless starving children), I prayed fervently for a bride doll.

"Why do you want one?" my mother asked.

"Because," was all I could say as I lay in the gutted bedroom where wall boards had been pulled loose and moist wood shavings tumbled free in order to dry. Wet shavings would swell and cause a fire, my father said.

Instead of praying for bride dolls, it was better to confess sins, my mother said, and then to try to make right the wrongs we did. And what about the crusts of bread I'd hidden behind furniture because I didn't want to eat them? I was told to think of those poor starving children and so that night I crawled beneath the bed and fished a crust of bread out from a corner and I ate it. Stinging pain sent me into my parents' room where, to their horror, my mouth lit up with the phosphorus glow of rat poison.

When I imagine myself as I was then, I see a slightly chubby person with legs as stocky as tree trunks, standing solidly in the middle of a tangled, confused yard. About me, in the ruined furniture and rotting lumber, is the reminder of chaos, an event which had turned our lives topsy turvey. But I can't remember the actual flooding of the river, I can only recall the immediate years after it, being warned not to touch any of the debris, to wash my hands thoroughly before meals, of things like diphtheria and having one's jaw locked shut. But the worst was the tearing down and re-building of our house.

When I look at photographs from around that time, I am usually wearing a white dress. The thick lenses of my glasses are heavy and they slide down my nose as I frown to keep them in place while I am forever peering out through the heavy blonde bangs of my over-grown butch cut. A shoemaker's children need shoes, my mother said, a butcher's, meat. And we were always in need of a hair cut. In most group photographs, I am either turned right around or looking off at something to the side of me. I was a sheet of jelly then, a hectograph, the old copier teachers used to prepare our work. They wrote on the gelatin with an indelible pencil (it was poison, we were warned not to chew on it). As the year progressed, the faint ghosts of past tests, the damp outlines of art work, criss-crossed, becoming a road map of the whole year.

Virginia never tanned or was affected by the sun in any way but my legs and face grew prickly and red in the hot wind. While we lay out there on the blanket, I wished I could climb above it, up where the vapour trails of jet planes arched into the sun, away from the whining of the electric saw and the hollow thud of a hammer echoing in the trees in the park as across a field, Mr. Pankratz finished building his new house.

Pankratz, the packrat, we'd named him because he'd built the house almost entirely from scrap. He'd paid little for the land because it bordered the edge of town and would be on the wrong side of the dike once it was in place. My father had branded him a "plain damned fool," but I didn't think he was that harmless. I walked in wide circles around the man to escape his clammy, pale hands which were forever reaching to pat my arm or the top of my head. In spring, my father said, water would back up from the river into the first and then the second park, flow across the road and completely surround Mr. Pankratz's house. So the man had built it up, had hauled in fill to raise the foundation as high as the level of the last flood. As a result, the house looked down over the whole town, the park, the bridge which spanned the Red River and the highway climbing to meet St. Mary's Road as it wound past Horseshoe Lake.

When Mr. Pankratz came to build our kitchen cupboards, my mother asked him why he had chosen to live there. "It must be terrible for mosquitoes," she said. And the park was a strange place in spring with oak trees standing in water, reflected back over and over. Once the water subsided, the ground remained soft and overnight, flesh-white toadstools, spongy and tall, sprung up from dampness. Virginia and I played down there. We told no one. The park floor was littered with flood-contaminated stock from the drugstore and off-limits. We played wedding. We collected toadstools and laid them out on wild rhubarb leaves for the wedding feast. Do you take this man as your lawful wedded husband? I asked. Do you take this woman to be your awful wife? Virginia would say, laughing, spoiling the ceremony. To her it was a game, the same as playing Dale Evans and Roy Rogers.

Mr. Pankratz removed his painter's cap and ran his hand across his smooth bald head when my mother asked him why he chose to build his house on the outskirts of town. He took his pencil out from behind his ear, squinted and said, "The town is for families. What would an old bachelor like me want in town?"

He's worse than an old woman, my mother complained because Mr. Pankratz liked to tell stories while he built the cupboards. He liked his new house, he told us. Know what he liked about it the most? My brothers and sisters and I were sitting on the floor around galvanized wash tubs, washing mud from my mother's canning sealers. I could see my mother's shoulders bunch with irritation. "I wouldn't know," she said.

"The indoor toilet," he said and set aside the board he was about to cut, freeing his hands to illustrate some point in the story with a bunched fist or a sweeping motion. He had been thinking that morning when he got up, what a good thing it was that he no longer needed to worry about digging another pit for the outhouse. The indoor toilet in his new house was the best thing. When he'd lived on the farm, of all the chores, he'd hated moving the outhouse most. When the lime had been dumped into the pit too often the ground all around the outhouse became spongy. He was afraid that someday he would step off the narrow plank and sink up to his knees. Then it would be up to him to dig another hole, move the outhouse onto it and fill in the other.

"The job came to me, every time," he complained. "I always did all the dirty work. Take David for instance," Mr. Pankratz said in a wounded voice to remind us of his sacrifice, how he had taken his sister's boy so she could be free to marry and move away to British Columbia and not have to live with the tragedy of David, who had stopped growing the day they discovered him up-ended in a water-filled rain barrel. "My sister has written only twice this year," he whined. "And I don't think she will even come to the wedding."

Throughout all the hammering and the sporadic whine of the electric saw, David sat on a chair outside, leaning against the house, blond head bent over his lap as he chipped and coaxed oddly shaped animals from blocks of wood his uncle had discarded. All the while, he smiled at something we couldn't see. When he walked, he seemed to feel his way along, as though he travelled through a dream.

"The bride chose a waltz-length dress, featuring a cumberbund and a lace bolero," Virginia read from the *Agassiz Herald*. What was waltz length? I wondered as I watched David's intense carving and Mr. Pankratz's struggle with a sheet of chalk board. Drywall, it is called now, but we called it chalk board because when it crumbled we salvaged pieces to draw our hopscotch on the sidewalks. Mr. Pankratz's house was new, but looked old. The roof had come from many roofs, the windows from the old school. And the style of it was like all the other old houses in Agassiz, like the one I lived in, a tall, two-storey house, windows arranged unimaginatively, two up and two down.

"You are welcome to come to the wedding of Lena Harms to David Pankratz, July 12, at 2 pm," the note read. There was no posting an announcement in the *Agassiz Herald* for this wedding. The announcement came in the form of a note delivered by a small child, which we were instructed to pass on from door to door. When my mother finished laughing, she let me read it. "Feel free to invite a friend. Come and bring your own refreshments," it said. The wording of the note had been the bride's mother's idea, Mr. Pankratz explained, his weathered cheeks flaring red. "She says in Paraguay, at a wedding, the whole village comes. For this reason, I thought it best we hold the affair at my place."

I had been inside the Harmses' house with Virginia when she went to collect for the newspaper and I agreed. The family had come from Paraguay the previous year. There had been gossip about the father and the family having been sent from the Mennonite colony because of something he'd done. They lived in a bricksiding cottage which had been badly flooded. You can't trust bricksiding, my father said. It doesn't let moisture escape and a house can look perfectly sound from the outside but be rotten to the core. The Harmses' house had three rooms for fourteen people. Along the walls, boxes filled with clothing were stacked one on top of another. The women of the town had collected the clothing when the family had disembarked at the train station in the dead of winter wearing only thin muslin. Each day, the children pulled what they would wear from the boxes. All around us in the cramped kitchen were children. They sat on the table, squatted on the floor, babies lay on a cot beside the stove, all dark-eyed, dark-skinned. One swung down from the top of the door and stared at us with lively eyes, eyes like the eldest, Lena's, the colour of black walnut. Dirty faces peered in at us through the window. When we'd come into the yard, we'd noticed a gas-powered washing machine standing idle and Lena bending over a pile of clothing on the ground. A kettle boiled on a hot plate.

No understand, no understand, the woman said in broken English. She pushed her feet into a pair of man's plaid slippers and took the kettle from the hot plate. We followed her outside with most of the children. Lena stood beside the washing machine on one foot, scratching at the back of her leg with the other. She was taller than her mother, slender, a strong nose, not the fleshy little ball of a nose that her mother possessed. For two days she'd sat behind me in school in a desk that was too small for her so that she had to turn sideways in it and her tanned, sandalled foot bobbed up and down in the centre of the aisle. Turn around, the teacher warned me when I couldn't stop staring. Lena's heavy black braids trailed down from her shoulders and lay against her full breasts. At recess, the boys turned rope for her so she could jump and they could watch her breasts bouncing beneath the paisley print dress. But she never knew. She skipped and laughed and you could tell she thought she was one of us.

Despite all the children, the jumble of clothing, I remember that the house was clean and the woman herself radiated the pleasant odour of oranges. Virginia and I explained why we had come. The woman and girl spoke to each other in Spanish. The mother frowned. No money, she explained. No money for anything. Not for gasoline. My husband, he take for his car, she said, ducking her head in a shy manner. She shouted to the children in Spanish and they came running with a pail. Gasoline, gasoline, they cried in high musical voices as they went from door to door.

But if the wording of the wedding letter had been the mother's idea, the marriage itself had been Mr. Pankratz's. He'd been walking down in the second park on the west side of the bridge where the trees were dense and it was cooler, he said. He'd looked up and saw David and the girl walking along the bridge. Why did she come every evening to lean on his fence and call for David? he wondered and had followed them, he told my mother, because he worried about David getting lost. And as he saw how she held David's hand, and how willingly he followed, the idea had come streaking down and "hit me like a bolt of lightning. Too soon oldt, too late schmart," he said. "I'm not getting any younger," he told my mother. "David needs someone to watch out for him."

"But is she able?" my mother asked. She shook her hands free of soap suds, slipped her wedding band back on and sat down for once, to listen. I wondered what her wedding dress had looked like. When I asked, she put me off, saying that it was not a regular dress, but pretty, and had buttons at the shoulder. There was no photograph of my parents' wedding in the album, although all her relatives were there in their matrimonial finery. There was only one photograph of them together and it was a surprising picture. My mother sat on my father's knee, bare legs exposed and on her feet, tiny pointed-toed shoes with bows. Her hair was longer than I ever remember her wearing it. She had swept it up behind one ear and the other side swung forward, a dark wedge against her white skin. A dark-haired Marlene Dietrich. She raised a glass to the person behind the camera. My father rested his chin on her shoulder and laughed. What was the occasion? I wondered. She didn't remember. A party of some sort. It was before, she searched for the words, before, she said. Before the flooding of the river? No, no, long before that. It was before I became a better person, she said without explaining.

"The mother says that in Paraguay they teach girls in school all things a woman should know," Mr. Pankratz said.

"Be that as it may," my mother said. "There's more to it than cooking and cleaning. She looks so young. She doesn't look any older than thirteen or fourteen."

"Sixteen," Mr. Pankratz said. The air was thick with sawdust and the warm smell of wood. A two-by-four thundered to the floor. "It's a good bargain for the girl to get her out of that place," Mr. Pankratz said. "And the mother sees it as well. It'll be one less mouth for her to feed."

My mother sighed. "Well, they will make a nice couple," she said. "Lena is a good-looking girl."

"He only wants someone to wash his dirty socks," she said when Mr. Pankratz had gone.

Virginia folded the newspaper and held it against her chest. The sun transformed dry patches on her arms into silvery scales. Virginia and I were best friends. She had Psoriasis and I, the coke-bottle eye glasses. "Dolores uses Kotex now," Virginia said. She scratched at her arms and blinked in the sunlight. Her eyes were always red-rimmed and sore-looking.

I didn't want to know what Kotex was but she took me inside the house which smelled sharply of aging varnish and cough medicine, a smell I thought came with their old house, but the odour had followed them here. Charlie Colpitts would walk a mile to get out of work, people said of Virginia's father and I associated the smell of the house with sloth. Mrs. Colpitts was a nurse at the hospital. She had scooped babies up from between legs, washed backs and bottoms and poked into bed pans and so people knew enough to leave the Colpittses alone. Mrs. Colpitts, Verna, was a short, sharp-featured woman with hair as stiff and unmanageable as Virginia's and Dolores's. She was the possessor of special knowledge. When I told her what my mother had said about Mr. Pankratz wanting someone to wash his socks, her face snapped to attention. His socks worsht, she said. Huh. As long as that's all he wants.

Virginia and I stood in Dolores's closet, examining a Kotex pad. "She puts it between her legs," Virginia explained. I resisted the explanation. I did not want to envision anything blotted or stained beneath satin skirts. "No, no," Virginia said. "They plan for that. They count the days so it won't happen."

The day of the wedding my mother sent me to Mr. Pankratz's house with a batch of buns. The sun had risen above the horizon which, beyond the shock of twisted oak trees in the park, was the stark horizontal line of St. Mary's Road. Above Horseshoe Lake, a veil of mist would be lifting and in the shallow ditches, ivory clouds of yarrow bobbed in a green sea. The bittersweet scent of a prickly rose bush growing thickly among the rusting shell of a car made my throat ache. As I walked, I remembered the same road muddy and slick after the flood and the sudden sound of rushing water stopping me dead. There, inches before my feet, the road fell away into a large hole. I stood mesmerized, watching with horror the yellow water roaring and tumbling beneath the road, carrying rocks and debris along with it. A temporary underground stream, my father explained but it didn't diminish the feeling I had of a world surging beneath my feet and I about to be swallowed and swept along underground with it.

I pictured my destination. I imagined that Mr. Pankratz had knocked lightly on the groom's door as he passed into the kitchen and heard the immediate, anxious reply of the bedsprings and then footsteps as David followed him into the kitchen. It was one of the "dirty jobs" Mr. Pankratz had explained to my mother, teaching David not to arise in the morning until he knocked. One winter David had wandered away from the house in his night clothes and suffered frost bite. I imagined the two men bent in silence over their breakfast plates, eating quickly, almost furtively, but as I entered the yard, I heard voices and came upon them behind the house on their hands and knees, weeding the garden.

"Already, visitors," Mr. Pankratz greeted me, scrambling to his feet. The glint of metal in the seat of his pants caught my eye. Once Mr. Pankratz had been crawling across a roof and split the seam in his trousers and he had used a length of stove-pipe wire to hold it together. Wired for sound, people joked. Old Pankratz doesn't want to miss a thing. Would the bride be required to mend his pants? From the park came the sudden scolding of a squirrel. Startled upright by the sound, David listened, a weed still clenched in his fist.

"Look who's here," Mr. Pankratz said to David, touching him to draw his attention. "Look what she brought." But David never looked at any of us directly. He seemed to be in another place, the place where his animal carvings took shape. From a fir tree at the back of the yard came the coo of a mourning dove. The sound was right for that time of day while the air was still cool and the dew had not yet been burned off by the sun. The sound was like gently moving air, like my mother's sigh.

I wondered what the bride was doing at that very moment. Mr. Pankratz had given the mother money to buy a dress, he'd said, so she would look half-decent. Was she awaking, stretching and yawning and seeing the dress, did her heart beat faster?

"Tell your Momma, thank you," Mr. Pankratz said. As he took the buns from me, his cool hands brushed against mine and I stepped back quickly, feeling in my mind his sticky touch on my arm. "Hurry, hurry," he said sharply to David as he carried the still-warm buns into the house. "They aren't going to be able to make their bachelor jokes about my garden today."

From across the field came the sound of Virginia's india rubber ball smacking against the cement and calling me to play.

The sun was hot and high in the sky, casting short, sharp shadows in the dirt of the yard when Virginia, Mrs. Colpitts and I crossed the field to the wedding. Mrs. Colpitts had allowed us to paint our nails for the occasion and I admired the poppy-red splashes on my hands. My mother, several of my sisters and brothers, and a few other women were already there. My father would not close down his barber shop to come. The only time he had ever closed his shop was when my oldest sister insisted on getting married on a Saturday, and then it was only for half a day. Mr. Pankratz and David had changed from their work clothes into white shirts and black pants. They sat on a makeshift bench, leaning against the house, waiting. And then, as though people had agreed to arrive at the same time, a line of cars travelled down the dirt road, slowly and almost silently. The brittle call of a crow down in the park grated at our silent expectancy. People came walking, carrying dishes and pans of food. Mr. Pankratz nodded his greeting to each one. The women, with quiet efficiency, began setting the food out on the table which Mr. Pankratz had made of plyboard and sawhorses. We strolled about the yard waiting for the arrival of the bride. Mr. Pankratz mopped his ruddy face and squinted at us from behind his handkerchief. Sit still, my mother cautioned. I sat on a chair and thought the people were like chickens, the way they glanced at David from the sides of their faces, advancing towards him so far, as though they might peck him on the leg, and then veering away quickly at the last moment. The way they craned their necks to peer down the road to see if the bride was coming. David whittled at a piece of wood, seeming not to notice any of us.

And then suddenly, everyone fell silent. Even the smallest ones paused in their restless games to see what was happening. My throat began to tighten. The crow flapped up from the trees in the park, laughing loudly as two smaller birds cried and darted about its head. At the top of the road, we could hear a flutter of sound, a light tinny clamour and then, growing louder, it became the voices of children singing. We all stood up. Down the road they came, the entire Harms family, barefoot children jumping around Lena in circles singing, "She's a bride, she's a bride. Lena is a bride." The older ones carried smaller ones on their hips. The parents each carried a bundle. Closer and closer they came, dancing and laughing and shouting in Spanish. My dress stuck to my back. My heart twisted at the sight of the bride and the pink flowers in her arms. Everyone stood motionless, staring, as single file, the family crossed the plank that spanned the ditch. David pulled at Mr. Pankratz's arm and smiled suddenly. "Lena," he said. "It's Lena."

"What the hell," Mr. Pankratz swore softly. "She didn't buy the girl a dress."

On Lena's blue-black head, attached with many pins, was an ivory lace curtain. Her dress appeared to be a bedsheet gathered at the waist with a man's necktie. The flowers were plastic and coated with dust. People moved aside to let the family pass through into the yard, carrying with them the smell of dust and heat and oranges. The mother stood before the groom, foxtail fur wound tightly about her neck. Above it, perspiration beaded her wide mottled face.

"I bring her to you," she said and dropped the bundle at his feet.

Mr. Pankratz stepped forward, his white hands on Lena's dark skin as he drew her towards him and led her over to David's side.

The father stood before them, grinning and nodding his approval. His dark hair, slicked straight back, shone with oil. "How you say. Good luck?" He looked to see if anyone appreciated his humour.

Lena's bold smile revealed large, straight teeth. She turned and spoke to two girls behind her who scrambled about arranging the curtain veil until it fanned out across the grass like a frayed fish tail.

I heard a sharp intake of breath. "Pity the poor thing." I thought I heard my mother's voice.

"Well, he's a better person than I to take the both of them on," a man said.

About me, I saw the evidence of laughter withheld in the flickering of muscles around mouths. Tears welled and spurted behind my glasses. "She's beautiful," I heard myself say. "The bride is beautiful."

Mr. Pankratz cleared his throat noisily. The women began to nod. "Yes of course, isn't she lovely?" someone said quickly.

"More than that. Every bride is lovely, but Truda is right, she is beautiful," my mother said as I ran from the yard crying.

"Well missy, what was that scene all about?" my mother asked. She removed her hat and set it down on top of the china cupboard. The cupboard stood in the centre of the dining room instead of its usual place against the wall beside the chimney. The linoleum had been ripped up from the floor, revealing the rippled floorboards beneath. Light filtering through the curtains made the air seem granular and grey. I imagined I could see molecules dancing in front of me. My mother had gone visiting after the wedding. As she set her hat down, a splash of gold sunlight rested on her cheek.

"A curtain," my mother said, not waiting for my reply. "Imagine. I think it was one of the things I sent over there." The floor boards groaned suddenly beneath our feet. A crack zigzagged up the wall behind her head. She frowned uneasily. My father had come home and gone into the basement to work. For weeks he'd been jacking the house up in an attempt to level the floors. Easy does it, he said. And little by little, the warped, twisted house was being straightened. The house groaned and china plates shivered in the cabinet. A chunk of plaster broke loose from the ceiling and scattered on the floor. "Oh Lord," my mother said. I was about to turn from the sight of it when my mother's hands flew up in front of her face. She shrieked. The china cupboard wobbled forward, dishes sliding together. Her shriek rose above the sound of shattering china as the cupboard crashed to the floor.

My father came running and stood in the doorway, red-faced and panting. "Is everything all right?" he asked.

My mother folded up and crumpled to her knees. "Is everything all right?" she cried. "Look, look at what you've done," she said and raising her hands to the cracked walls, the crumbling ceiling, she began to cry.

My father stepped forward and then flung the crowbar he'd been carrying across the room. "It was an accident, for God's sake, Mika," he said. "It's only dishes. I thought it was something serious."

My mother's voice cracked. "But it was all I had," she said. "It was all I had left."

My brothers and sisters stood gaping. I left the house. My mother's cries were as birds' wings churning the air about my head as I ran down the road. Breathless and chilled, I leaned against the red barn, my back warmed by heat trapped in the weathered boards. I waited until the china scraps were gathered and scattered into the garden and the cabinet thrown on top of the heap of rubble in the back of the yard. I waited beside the red barn until I saw them later on, before my sister came calling and searching for me. The wedding couple walked among the trees in the park in their wedding clothes, two pale ghosts moving among the purple shadows, a flutter of silver and white. The following day, in the heat of high noon, they stood beside the road, waist-deep in the bobbing yarrow, holding hands, and smiled at me. Another evening, I saw them out by Horseshoe Lake while thunder rolled over the cattails and the air hung thick with the scent of a storm. And one night as I watched from a window in my tall narrow house, the groom held the bride's veil high as they walked up and down the streets of town and no one laughed. Below them in the flood-littered park, for a fractured second, among the toadstools a lady slipper glowed, singly and silent.

KATE BITNEY

Noon And My Sisters

Noon   and my sisters
inhabiting the hill   become
transparent as ice   against
the hot high sun

My sisters   holding one
another's hand   float downward
on the slopes
stepping sweetly   heads together
their harmless hair   tangles
in the upsweep of the air

My moaning sisters blow
pathways in the long grass
with their feet   they journey
to the coast of night
become

spear and crossbow
enemies of men

I Am Shown The Land

I ask for a vision
I am shown the land:

the humped bum of hills,
bright the belly of lake

and eye of big round moon;
tongue of cactus

rakes the ground yellow, hollow

marks me down as
clover, mustard: fallow.

But that is not enough:
the land's eye roves
with the cunning of

the circling sun
devours the fields

of stragglers, feeds
their flailing spirits

to the solemn wind
to make it richer, more velvet,

swifter to push shadows
over hills, to silken,

stroking the backs
of fields, hair

of saskatoonberry
hands of water

twisted leg of road.

Someday, daughter,
all this will be yours
(limbs of poplar,
bendy, true

eyes of roadside slough
pupils of mallard, mallow)

Stop motorbikes, cars,
erase oil

put all the gravel back
to where it was.

Return electric
to the exciting air.

ruling his shrunken kingdom from a wheelchair
my father peels potatoes in his withered
women's lap his forty years dominion over
every living thing comes only to this playing
cook's helper in my mother's kitchen his
mighty furrowed thousand acres contracted so
suddenly to her modest garden plot we are
made breathless by this hasty engagement
the shocking imprudence of a sick man's match
it isn't so far from what he would have wished
sitting in the sun on his mother's ancient
weathered wooden bench thinking old men's
thoughts & yet he holds through this indecent
bedding down to the lawful words of his old
command & she continues to obey while under
our desperate family charade his thick fingers
fumblingly caress these earth brown globes
learning gropingly to say the silent love words
of his abdicating

i wish the sky was still pasted on
to the ceiling the floor of God's
heaven i wish the stars were really
made of tin foil sliding at night
into dark earth under my bed i want
angels in cellophane surrounding my
head i want the old jesus with his
tin lantern & his sheep knocking
knocking at my wooden door i want
crashing alone into this black river
someone beside me the old old clutch
still at my soul

& i what do i want in this my contradictory
most treacherous false heart of hearts
i want you passionate steed sword & bridle
gleaming the hero still to carry me away
with your longing capture me in your flaming
eternal all knowing yes in spite of everything
the women the teacups the wine sitting together
here in this room speaking our independence
our new vision what i want is the old promises
all the ironies swept away Cinderella rising
from the ashes glassy eyed her empty face
her transparent shoes

Diana

i used to have a lot of trouble with my name   in Reinland
where i grew up people named their children Peter & Agnes &
Sara & Jacob   in fact there was so much duplication of
names you might find yourself in the position of say Peter
Peters son of Peter Peters son of Peter Peters   this wasn't as
confusing as it sounds   there wasn't a lot of mail & the
identities of fathers & sons were not that clearly distinguished
anyway   most of the time you referred to people by their
nicknames which everybody knew like Schwauta Petasch
or Boaut Jaunzen   what was an exotic name like Diana
doing in a plain village like Reinland   not only did it
lack the resonance of a long line of aunts & grandmothers it
was hard for people to say   they would roll it around on
their tongues tasting its foreignness & then spit it out   a
friend of my grandfather's once asked me aren't you terribly
depressed to have a name like that   my mother's cousin
Susch was undaunted by it   she would hug me tight on her
lap & tickle & squeeze me with her crippled hand all the while
crooning Diantche oba Diantche oba Diantche   later my
brother & sister would follow me around mercilessly chanting
Diantche oba Diantche   part of the joke was it sounded a lot
like little duckling little duckling in Low German   we didn't
get to read books much   the school library was a tiny
cupboard in the corner of the room   you could read through
the entire collection in half a year & you only got to switch
rooms every four years   the public library which came to
town once a month in a van was forbidden to us on grounds
of worldliness   but we did get to hear a fantastic array of
Bible stories   i was fascinated by their exotic foreign
flavour   they always came with a moral attached at the end
which would relate them to our own plain little world but it
never came close to capturing their beauty & terror   it was

extremely hard to see for example how the point of a story like the multicoloured Joseph in Egypt being seduced by Potiphar's wife could possibly be that we shouldn't tell lies to our parents   i did find one story which i felt i could claim for my own   my second name is Ruth so i paid particular attention to Ruth the Moabite who followed her mother in law home & worked in the fields with her   her faithfulness made her belong in spite of her foreign past   your people shall be my people & your God shall be my God   i clung to this story as a way of getting through the other passage from the Bible which had to do with me whenever the minister in church read about the heathenish Diana of the Ephesians & the wickedness she caused among God's people i modestly lowered my head & tried to look Ruthlike   i even told my teacher once to call me Ruth from now on   she smiled indulgently & instantly forgot   later in high school i discovered other more interesting stories about the goddess whose name i bore   Greek myths were okay to read as long as you didn't mix them up with the Bible   they were strictly classical references to explain the strange names strewn so improvidently through English literature which we had to read to get through Grade 12   i found out that she was a huntress & a moon goddess both of which suited me fine   there weren't any forests around our farm but i could easily imagine gliding among trees in buskins & i was on intimate terms with the moon already   a ghostly galleon tossed upon cloudy seas   she was also the virgin goddess which worried me a lot during the time my twin sister Rosie & her friends were going on heavy dates & i was sitting at home vascillating between the terror of acquiring breasts & periods & the shame of getting them so late   i liked the story of Actaeon who was turned into a stag for spying on Diana   it was a thrill to think of being able to turn boys' tricks inside out like that   by this time my friends were calling me Di which i liked because it was short & neat & it turned every greeting into a little song   hi Di bye Di   the only problem with it was meeting new people who would usually raise their eyebrows & say oh you mean Diane & even if i emphasized the *a* at the end of Diana they would still invariably spell it with a double *n* or some other unforgivable mistake   this problem was solved miraculously for me a few years ago by his royal highness Prince Charles   he couldn't know of course that his choice of the future Queen of England would personally affect the identity of a missing Mennonite peasant girl from Reinland   but it did   since the advent of Lady Di no one has ever questioned my name   in fact it has given me my own modest taste of royalty   a five year old girl at Victoria Albert school in Winnipeg came up to me one day & said i saw you on tv   what was i doing on tv i asked her much surprised   getting married she said   to Prince Charles   so i felt like a princess for one day   going back to Reinland now i notice several young Dianas swinging in the school yard & skipping in the ditches   nothing feels as separate as everything once did   it's hard to tell anymore what is exotic & what is plain   i like it that way

LOIS BRAUN

The Edge of the Cornfield

"Don't hang up." The words are quick and breathless, spoken even before the receiver is at my ear. "Don't hang up. Please." But I do hang up, without saying hello. Not angrily, not with that sharp crack of smooth, hard plastic on steel, but gently and—almost—regretfully. I must hang up, because of what you said the first time you called. A stranger, and yet your words make me afraid you are someone who knew me once. But it is impossible.

It is the fourth call. They're never at the same time of day, or of the week, and sometimes the voice sounds far away, as though he is calling from underneath the sea, which is far from here. The voice, no matter how distant, fondles and cloys, even in such few words as he is able to say before I cradle the telephone receiver, "...don't hang up...."

They told me not to come here, to these two old rooms in this old building that smells of fish and camphor all the time, and smells of fish and camphor here, now, though I am sprinkling leaves of rosemary into the sauce bubbling on the stove.

The hallways are painted the colour of a tropical ocean after a hot, oily rain, and it is this heavy, oriental sea-colour that seems to exude the smells of fish and camphor. The fluorescent glare of my windowless kitchen tries to burn away the alien sounds and odours and textures of this old ruin so far from my clean, green fields. On these streets, in these two rooms, I ache with time passing, and my phantom lover's calls knell the hours like a tower clock. Look at my fingers, gone white and wrinkled like the corner-store cabbage. The dull edge of the knife is the dullness of my own mind.

I used to eat my meals by the window in the other room, the window where neon beer signs across the way turned the red of my wine from titian to indigo to scarlet, over and over, flavouring my simple food with colour, making rich the sun-starved fruits of plastic gardens. And through the windows I'd watch the people under the beer signs, people who were smudges on the dirty pane, and by the way the smudges moved I was able to decipher their moods. And when it rained and streaks of clean glass allowed me to peek at their faces, there was no one there to see, because it was raining.

But now I must stay away from windows. I will dine at the kitchen cupboard, facing a photograph of an old woman who warned me not to go. She does not call me. My mother has brushed me away without a thought, like cobwebs out of corners in spring.

There is French jazz on the radio, azure tones that permeate my skin and play my nerves like harp strings. I turn out the lights in the two rooms, and when I go to my bed, I nearly forget to check the lock on the door, the old door with the old-fashioned skeleton key, a fitting key. How many other keys like it drift from one man's hand to another in the city outside?

Just before I fall asleep, I remember the way my collie, after years of tender nipping and pouncing, finally with no warning clamped his jaws on the back of my tortoiseshell cat, his lifelong companion.

Is the caller someone I know?

The buzz of my alarm clock is not like a telephone bell, yet half in sleep, I spring out of bed and blunder with sand-filled eyes towards the kitchen wall. I pull the receiver to my mouth, I shout, "Hello? Hello?" It takes several seconds before I know no one is there. I stand several seconds longer with the earpiece pressed to my cheek while voices from outside and from the corridor filter through my sleep and my dream, and it comes to me that it is morning. Shouts of play-bound children and angry mistresses jab at me through the keyhole of the apartment door.

The dusty sitting-room window lets in some light, and I dare to stand by it for a moment. Certain shadows and reflections I've come to know tell me there is sun this morning. I will not need my umbrella today.

While the old woman watches me pick through a shabby jar of olives to find just one more that still has its jewel-like centre, a telephone rings. I concentrate on my searching, and try to imagine it is the phone in the next apartment. But the ringing is coming from my telephone. He's never called in the morning. It could be—someone else.

He says my name. This time I drop the receiver into the cradle. It is a shard of ice that numbs my fingers. He knows my name. He knows who I am.

I *must* go to work. I must go to work to keep my daily appointment with the skew-mouthed, firm-fleshed boy who buys sweet, raw Brazil nuts from my uncle's stall every morning at eleven when he finishes jogging across the Mid-town Bridge and back again. I've seen him only when his hair is sticky and limp, his face wet from exertion. But I watch him buy his paper cup of honeydew from the stand across the promenade, and then he comes to my stall—my uncle's—and I look at his eyelashes, which are longer than any I've seen on the few men I've really looked at up close.

He does not look at my face.

I pour the olive dregs down the toilet, and put on my Mary Quant hat, which might be a disguise, though Uncle would frown if he dropped in at the stall today. He has instructed me to wear white blouses and keep my hair pinned back from my face so that I will look "fresh and clean and crisp, like kohlrabi."

Half-way through the morning, it begins to rain. No one comes to buy. Some of the concessions close up. I keep my stall open, in case the boy comes, and stare at the honeydew stand across from me. Soon, a man wearing a suit and carrying a black umbrella that covers his face comes to buy pumpkin seeds, and while we listen to the dull plopping of the raindrops on the umbrella, the man gives me some coins. But they aren't enough, and when he gropes for the wallet in his back pocket, his jacket moves aside and I see something shining silver above his belt, like the handle of a gun. I take the bill too nervously from his soft hand, wishing I had taken the coins he'd offered first, and in my haste knock the bags of seeds to the wet ground. He picks them up, and as he walks away I see him wiping the muddy package against his sleeve, as though perhaps they are to be a gift for someone.

Still, I watch for the boy, and so compressed am I into that one expectation, I do not wonder at all that a faceless man carrying an umbrella and a gun would come to buy pumpkin seeds on a rainy morning.

I shutter the stall, finally, and walk in the direction of the bridge, past the cement park, past the relic steam engine that looks as if it's been still-framed in a vintage film, past the red-brick houses with the wrought-iron gates. A figure darts out from a side street, running, and I freeze. But it is only someone hurrying to get out of the rain.

And now, the streets seem to be full of people running. I hear the clatter of flat-bottomed running shoes on the drenched pavement all around me. One of them will be him, on his way from the bridge to buy Brazil nuts. I picture him now, very wet, with his clothes and hair clinging so that he is sleek and thin and shimmering. But the clatter is merely the intensity of the rain, falling harder now in bigger, heavier drops.

I turn to go back, but as I glance at one of the brick houses, I see a figure of a man. He is in a second-storey window and he is watching me. A man in a suit is watching me through the downpour of grey. His hand moves, perhaps to wave to me, or to reach for something.

Beneath him, in front of the door, sits a cat, its fur flattened and dark, its ears drooped and bent to keep out the raindrops, and I can just make out a wretched lump of mouse at its feet.

The apartment building where I live is so quiet in the afternoon. Even the street outside is empty as I hurry, stiff with cold, from the bus stop a block away. Today, the corridor oozes its viscous colours and odours into the air around me, and as I twist my thin key in the lock, I think, for the first time in years, of cornfields.

When I was younger than ten, both in years and in living, I ran through cornfields unafraid, knowing that in any direction lay an edge of open space where I could get my bearings and find my way home. Mother was not always there when I arrived at the back door with my straight yellow bangs stuck to my forehead. She made brief escapes often in those days, and I, safe in cornfields, believed in the necessity of her many excursions, usually to the city. I could not, then, have recognized her loneliness; I thought she complained too much, and that she knew too little of the outside world that was Father's and mine. It was this world, Father's and mine, that her bitter voice would infiltrate late at night while I lay in bed straining to hear Father's soft-spoken answers.

One autumn, while I was playing in sunshine, feeling warm and fine, Mother bought a fur coat. Not an expensive one, not mink, and it was "slightly used," smelling faintly of moth-balls. But she had saved up the money for it, then mended it and "spiffed it up" at her sewing machine in the kitchen corner where she also kept her books. She could not sew very well. We admired the coat, with its dark, rich sheen, the aura of glamour with which it enveloped the plain woman in the kitchen.

As autumn harvest drew on into shorter and shorter days, days of chill, white skies, Mother slipped as undiscernibly and as surely as those days into her own kind of winter. One day after school I found her flitting about the house. When she saw me, she scolded about a ribbon I'd lost from one of my braids. Then she told me she was going out and wouldn't be home until late. She dressed up nice and wore her fur coat.

As Father and I worked in the grain bins that evening, it began to snow, huge, sloppy flakes that made a sizzling noise when they landed on the dusty, dry yard.

When I went back to the house alone, I found it the way I'd left it, except that a glow of light shone from Mother's sewing corner. The sewing machine cabinet was open, and Mother was slumped over on it, still wearing her coat. Her head rested on the soft fur of her sleeve, and one of her hands curled protectively around a glass of Father's whiskey. There was nothing else on the cabinet—no bit of mending, no new ribbons for my braids. Her eyes were closed and she was very still, but I'd never seen Mother sleep and couldn't tell whether or not she was sleeping then. But it was the coat that surprised me most. The fur was wet and stuck down, almost matted, as though she'd stood for a very long time in the snowfall, perhaps right outside the bin where Father and I had hammered nails into fresh clean boards. The sheen on the coat was no longer glamorous, and the smell of camphor was strong in the room.

In my child's mind, I trusted Father to take care of this unusual circumstance; but in a deeper, older part of me, I learned on that day that my mother was not safe in cornfields, and in the autumn that followed, I played in them less and less.

I didn't see the coat again until the morning of my father's funeral, when I saw Mother go to her closet and briefly finger the hem of the sleeve. She never wore it again.

She watches me from the photograph, older than her years, older than she wanted to be, older than she thought she could ever become. She always came back in those early years, but now I've left her, and though I expect to see her again one day, she's already brushed me away, knowing that *she* never wanted to come back. Staring at her picture, I feel a slow-moving peril creeping towards me from a great distance, that great distance beneath the sea, and it occurs to me all at once that I have not taken a breath for a long time. The air is so heavy, and though I sit very quietly, and there is no other sound, I sense someone in the hall coming towards my door. At first, the sensation is not strong enough for me to react. But the wave finally touches shore and I turn to look at the door, at the doorknob, and at the keyhole, and again I remember that the door is not locked. I steal across the room and take my key from the top of the refrigerator, and just as I insert the key in the lock, I feel—I am sure—another key enter from the other side. And as I twist the key, the other key twists the opposite way. It wants to unlock an unlocked door. The metal strains behind the brass plate. I press my forehead to the door-frame and funnel my energy into the key. A key must break, mine or his. Then I feel the other withdraw, as if my opponent has had a change of heart. My key completes the turn and the bolt clicks conclusively in the latch.

At night I dream of a man in a suit pacing his room while staring at a large, emphatic telephone on the desk by his bed. He paces and paces and swears in an unearthly dialect that needs no translation, so expressive is it in its curious blends of sounds and rhythms. He paces and paces, and then, with cold precision rather than uncontrolled rage, he takes a silver-handled gun from his belt and shoots at the telephone many times. The bullets travel slowly from the gun to the telephone, and though they are large and the shots echo as in a vault, the telephone does not shatter, nor even crack or bend. My place in the dream is unclear, perhaps that of a voyeur.

In this morning of invisible sun, I emerge from sleep chanting ancient numbers like a long-lost charm retrieved from the bottom of a well. I press my fingertips to the telephone dial for a few moments before defining the code that will reach at last beyond these barriers towards the familiar, clean, green fields. And there, it is her voice, coming from far away. And I am not sure at first if she is really saying my name, here and now, or if it is simply another phantom seeking to violate me in some terrifying and intimate manner. But the third time she says my name, I hear the beginning of panic rising in her voice, and I know that I must speak, so that we may begin, finally, to make our way out of the cornfield, to find the edge, to find out if it is still there.

Fielding

(for my father)

"Thanks for everything" you quietly tell us
boldly for you who never knew quite how to
say such things with any ease
as we load our girls and luggage
into the car heading once more back to Winnipeg
and you pack your coffee and science fiction
into the cardboard box that is to see you
through the day watching alone
over a monstrous claw that
needs only the iron bones to rise
rigid behind it to rip off the overburden
sandy earth in abandoned fields
sealing the darkness sown 40 feet beneath us

where driven by thistles and dust
you spent your prime
stood knee deep in water
steeping in those strange long holes
punched coal from layers of packed clay
picking fire out of gleaming black seams

no place for any man
certainly no place for a young man like you
tempered to life by a thin white disc
that scraped inside your lungs   gently
with its sharp metal breathing

that was no place for you to be   father
far below the wasted prairie slamming its way
above you / above you
the baseball diamonds you told me about
where Clarey Weir ran 5 miles
from his father's dairy farm every game
to catch pop-ups in his hip pocket
and Barney Krivel swung under liners
in centre field with his back to the plate
and where you yourself pasted baseballs
through the Thirties / your twenties
using that ridiculous stubby glove i found
in the attic on the farm one day

you a sunburned farmer born to the prairies
held hard to the place
holding in the peak of your firm strength
those smooth wooden bats and angular picks
like they all did   all the men who stayed on
stood swinging at the round blurs
firing white past them
knelt digging in lignite
crumbling pockets of brown carbon

i remember you
years later in the white light
bent on our 55 Massey
dragging the rusted discer
over Evendon's section 7 miles north of town
its steel plates glinting on the rub of dirt
and the loud sudden scrape of rocks
grinding off sparks
your striped engineer's cap ruling the redness
in a clean line across your forehead

(the startling white softness of your body
underneath the gray cotton shirt you always wore)
and the sweet smell of the soap and cream
you pulled through the zipper of
your pebble-grained leather shaving kit
on Saturday nights and how in good spirits
we rolled down the gravel road
over the big hill under
the orange slant of the sun
with Hank Snow blowing us down into Estevan
from CHAB in Moose Jaw yellow
on the radio of our '53 green Ford
Just to think it could be
Time has opened the door
And at last I am free
I don't hurt anymore
and how the new mercury vapour street lights
would take us in their blueness past
the dazzling forkclinks and the lemonhalibut smells
fanning from the Canada Cafe
direct to the onoffonoffon incandescence drawing us
dreaming into the deep violet shade of the Orpheum theatre
where for 15 cents we witnessed
Gene Autry "the singing cowboy"
rescuing forlorn women in flickering melodrama

now the sunburn has almost gone from your neck
and the blackness is receding from your hair
but your hardened wrists
still thicken and move
after all these years
as we shake hands
and we see again
the light that has always sat / sits now
in the brown of your eyes
the slight halt that rests in your words

shapes of frost

leaning against August the fall corn   in full kernels ripened
until the first frost of September   chewed fast like fat whitebugs
into the sun-flower fainting in the sky   and slumping over in the fields

so earth exposes   its chilly cheeks
and wan October in a huff pours big bottles of gin into the hurry of wind
rubs the rouge off   the moon's warm mouth
flaking pigment off its face   powdering and pock-marking it
then Hallowe'en shoving over half-ton toilets   and shaving off the tan of stubble
hoarfrost hurdling the fences   hurts the garden huddled on hard ground

and then the bright air   froze to aethered feathers
the farthered sky anaesthetized   summer's sweaty stab
so stiff ropes of water   grabbed at the gabled roofs
cabled their coldness   close along kitchen walls
and coal pails   piled in the porch
Christmas cobbling joints of cold   bolting them into beams and joists
January grappling quebec heaters   gobbling their hot flutter of guts
and February fisted its frost   fingering and unfastening windows and floors
winter nailed so hard into studs   the cat froze solid in the oven one night
and so babies bagled warm in bed   woke blinking to the bright white
shapes of frost   heavy silhouettes folded
upon their lines of dark   around their lanes of dreams

corvus brachyrhynchos

a chunky bird
related to the blue jay and the magpie
totally black except for
a blush of bluish or greenish sheen
concentrated on its wings back and tail
its bill and feet are strong and black
the eye is dark

an opportunist in its feeding
it will eat almost anything
weed seeds garbage grasshoppers field mice baby birds frogs
oats gophers crickets dead skunks ducks eggs dogs on manure
piles plums humps of fat corn ants snakes live and dead sunflower
seeds squashed porcupines chopped off chicken heads cow pies
run over cats frozen robins starved meadowlarks rats diseased
orioles grounded spiders cows entrails pig shit cold porridge
steers testicles horse buns capsized pigeons stored wheat rotten
pumpkins blue flies bean sprouts washed up fish slow mice
run over weasels mangled gophers stale bread spoiled potatoes
sick kittens slugs rabbits grapefruit rinds squirrels with broken
necks kidneys of lame horses lungs of tubercular sheep turnips
left in gardens carrot peelings young chickens ladybugs fresh
dog turds stale dog turds fishflies saskatoons acorns chestnuts
cheese afterbirth skunks smeared on roads eyes is especially

fond of eyes
in legend and in fact
it pecks out the eyes of hanged men
almost anything that catches its eye

highly adaptable and resourceful
is capable of occupying
a great variety of habitats
it even scrounges on the fringes of cities
in the winter congregates
around garbage dumps and slaughter houses
where its coarse shouts can always be heard
above the other birds

much maligned as a nest plunderer
"a dozen nests may be found
occupied one day and destroyed the next"
and tormenter of pet dogs
is intelligent and gregarious
a skilled mimic it can learn to speak
and invariably it makes a most affectionate and entertaining
pet when domesticated

by the red

by the red river
river so low
walk by the willows
feel the rains blow

feel the slow rains dear
feel the rains flow
september mornin
cold rain like snow

if you cant call now
call when you can
warm in your voice love
glad in your hands

you at my window
you at my door
hold me once more dear
hold me once more

leave you a letter
leave you this song
leave you my love dear
sayin so long

send me some words though
though they are numb
words to remember
when they will come

willows of green leaves
sprinklers of sun
spindles of air love
whiskey of sun

crow in a door dear
crow in a door
hungry for somethin
wont see you no more

so pay me no visit
pay me no heed
sun starts to rise
sun starts to bleed

headingly jail love
headingly jail
think of me penny
in headingly jail

by the red river
river so low
walk by the willows
blowin in snow

dear valentine

in february
                when the cold cruises past
like a pet gander
                    in snuffle of wind
when afternoon light
                        stumbles over the house
& the moon
                elbows propped on the window
shimmy-shuffles in to our room
                                on cold hens feet
mercury curls in on himself
                            like an intestine
the tungsten frost
                    shunts the sky
like boxcars startled awake
                            & night
ratchets down on us
                        with a buzz

& you home
                in yr red toque
leaning like a speedskater
                            into the torque of wind
home at last
                in toque & tongue

then you
my love you are
the stove
thaws my rad
you are
the pump oils my threads
you are the oil can
melts my rust

day hardens

till its stuck & then
stiffens to toffee

night slouches in & the dark
the dark flows in

& begins
to grow/ glow in yr fingers
what do you see
moon an ice cube
floating in rum
& the moon slippery
in her mouth
a cinnamon candy once

the thots clog up
behind eyeskin
as if they were
breaks filling up with blood
or dogs/ shaken

dont take my love lightly

so you listen to the night
cars wriggle past in worms of light
stars stare at you
they are beads helixing time
) that night penny with the choker
on her neck
ohh ohhh
the stars on her neck then
warm from her body

just now
the wind shivers &
you can overhear
electric crackings in
blue tissues
a cap
crinkling over
head

then blind
sloughing the last skin of night
peeling it off
like her dress
the chest of skin breathing
hard
hhaa haa
when they slide
2 x 4 s of sun
inside my cell

morning gulping
bottles of night

wet pain in our mouth
& the sky
coughing blood

Travelling Back

pulled
pale from our guilt
he comes
at last undressed

pressed from me
my brother
unravels
he flies
a thread through
the eye of sun
strung out to dry

that is why my brother
now he has cooled
unspools the knots of fear
purled out of him
he is a sweater
he comes undone

but soon sun will unsky
will run and treadle
a needle trying
the skin on my need
a pin to ease the pain

I will prepare
for then when
thin and bare-footed
he will come
John in his beard
so spare
and his hands his

smooth smooth hands
he will come again
quite quietly he will
sliver my sight
oh then we will patch our guilt together
my brother and I
unspoil this shiver of night

he forever and ever
my John
and we this time
will silver the guilt
thick on my bed
thick as the quilt
teasing it out
and we
we dissolving
the sin wet so wet
and so sweet in our mouth

CHESTER DUNCAN

Up and Down in the Depression

Those of us who have done nothing for the revolution that has transformed our country except survive it, remember the Hungry Thirties as the social equivalent of the private pains of growing up. Nevertheless, these were the only years in our lives when we became famous in book and story—not in a personal way, but as a group. The unemployed and the semi-employed and the pretending-to-be-employed were the impersonal and convenient heroes of that time. They didn't give us anything, but they wrote articles about us.

Every day you'd pick up the paper and read about the economics of the situation, which were always fairly encouraging, and every day on the street and in the business building you'd encounter the shame of being a third-class citizen, one without a job. People would look at you, instinctively recognizing your jobless condition, just as blacks are looked at in the Deep South. Either they resented the eyesore, or you weren't really there. Every day you'd scan the want-ad pages filled with marvellous opportunities for being a radio-expert or a salesman. At one point I became attached to a door-to-door project for selling midget vacuum-cleaners, and after the first dreadful week of that I had to placate the firm by buying one myself, reducing my nest-egg (left by my family) by a third.

Even for a petit bourgeois like myself the late Thirties were really hungry. Extreme thinness is generally not unrelated to hunger. I remember a particularly healthy, particularly ebullient, particularly disagreeable elder of our church striding along the street on the strength of a full stomach and seeing me there—just barely there, looking like a beggar but too proud to be one—and exclaiming: "Are you feeling all right?" When I miaowed a feeble *yes thanks*, he said, "Oh, that's all right then; I thought by the look of you you might be in a decline—but that's all right then." And with these reassuring words he raced away to the prayer-meeting.

I remember a few weeks later he arranged a treat for me by taking me out to play a short service for the poor unfortunate prisoners at Stony Mountain Penitentiary—hymns and so on—and after the short service this pious man asked me to play for the congregation, who looked at this point absolutely in despair, and I played a Chopin Prelude for them, a very short tragic one. My elder friend, taken a little aback at the brevity of the piece, said breezily, "Well, that's the way you like it boys, isn't it, short and sweet!" The boys didn't answer.

At any rate we ate quite well that day, at the penitentiary, and I began to toy with the idea of becoming a prisoner by some satisfying crime, preferably of passion. On the other day, the day this good man said I was in a decline and that I mustn't work so hard, I hadn't been working at all for months. I hadn't eaten much for some time, and nothing at all that day.

Those of us who survived the Thirties hate with all our hearts the question "How are you?", although its genial offshoot, "Well, how are you anyway, you old obscenity obscenity?" is O.K. But the serious or probing *how are you?* is a key to cupboards full of skeletons to anyone who is sensitive to the carnal truth in himself. The truth of one's physical condition was always on one's thin hunched shoulders or in one's gnarled fists in those days. There were always those who delivered the seemingly kind question in the subtle tones of cruelty, so that at best *how are you* sounded like "Are you sure you ought to be out in weather like this?" or "Are you taking care of yourself?" At such moments life seemed to me to be very much a callous, competitive affair of, if not the elimination, at least the bare survival of the unfit, whose physical misfortunes gave a faint pleasure even to their friends.

Actually I wasn't nearly as badly off as some were. I could for example imagine myself as a remittance man—the romantic black sheep of the family who had to be appeased by regular handouts—for I received $17 every month from overseas to pay for my room. I was about as far from being a black sheep as it is possible to be, although I was rather sheepish. Such dreams, such games, however, I found useful in the business of survival.

This was the high dream: the low dream was the game of dividing up the quarters and dimes so that a pretence of three meals a day could be maintained. The question often was whether to dare to spend more than 10 cents on breakfast and do with soup for lunch. Or in the evening, instead of a full-course meal for 25 cents at a shabby-genteel restaurant, to have a full-course meal at a crummy joint for 15 cents, with a little left over for a heavenly all-day sucker or an Eatmore bar.

Into the blessed haven of the crummy joint I often saw enter one of the lost and neglected, and he would order a cup of coffee (5 cents). Into the coffee would go spoon after spoonful of sugar, and then as he drank the brew he would fill it up again and again with cream, so by the tolerance of the management and the real plentifulness of food he would tank up to the extent of between 700 to 1000 calories. It was lucky that the class to which I belonged as a remittance man in society prevented my following suit, because I'd never have had the nerve.

After a few years I had more money than that anyway—enough actually to keep alive on and save a little, so that at least once a week I could see a movie (costing generally 20 cents). In the late Thirties the state of the world was so bad that there was nothing for it some nights after reading the newspaper but a good double-feature.

One always needs something, of course, to get through the day. In those bleak times it was the double-feature, gay, interminable, and foolish. Now it's probably mostly television, for those who prefer it to liquor. As every social worker knows, or should know, the one piece of furniture that never should be pawned or sold in every doomed household, is the television set. Those whom God and Canada have forsaken must have the television (it used to be the movies) if only to keep them quiet. So that if the father of a slum household happens to be a drunken fool and the mother a sloppy termagant and there is nothing ahead of the children but a swamp in which to sink, one can at any rate get a TV set in there somehow. Extravagance is necessary in all desperate situations, but especially if you are desperately poor.

That is only one of the things that poverty can teach you, but sometimes the lesson that is harshly learned has a varying effect in the future. For instance I know that some of my contemporaries in the Depression were so hard-up that poverty made them penny-pinchers, conscious ever afterwards of a pathological attachment between themselves and money; whereas to others, like myself, the experience of having nothing only sharpened the joy and the freedom of becoming employable later on. I mean that it was very pleasant indeed to have money ten years later, but not to keep it. It was only that one need never worry about it again.

To return to some of the conditions of those formative years—I mean formative in the sense of blows to the head and kicks in the belly. I was desperately trying to make a living in music, but the local attitude to mildly talented home-town boys, though emotionally generous, was prudentially controlled when it came to payment. Everyone felt that I must have more experience before I was ready.

However, I did get to play the piano at a good many banquets and luncheons of the Kiwanians and Rotarians and Moose and Goldeyes and so on, and in the midst of these sadly enthusiastic ceremonials there was always food, and sometimes a little money too if one was playing for an assisting artist generous enough to share her five bucks with you. Nowadays of course you'd be lucky to get the same performance—I mean the same bad singing and bad playing of bad songs ("Ah Rose Marie I Hate You" and Mana-Zucca's "I Loathe Life: I Want to Die")—under thirty bucks. But in 1936 it was different. Some years later a friend and I decided to take our revenge on the past by somehow arranging to play piano duets at a service club luncheon, and when the assembled company was trying to digest the meal to the accompaniment of the fancy, inaccurate, and jocular introductions by the program convenor and expecting to hear some classical piece like *La Cucaracha*, my friend and I spread out the score of a Haydn symphony and played the whole thing from beginning to end (it took about half an hour), after which the meeting broke up in some dismay. Some of the members hadn't known that there existed pieces that long.

Playing for one's supper or one's lunch was quite 18th century in a way, although I never really felt the crunch of an artist's humiliation until the time I was actually hired (for 10 dollars) by a rich man to accompany his visiting cousin, a rotten singer from Chicago, at a party in the rich man's mansion in Tuxedo. He said that I was to wear my tuxedo, to fit the occasion, but when I got there I was put in the servants' quarters and brought out at the appropriate time without being introduced to the guests. The rotten singer from Chicago had a huge pile of music, nearly all bad, and he sang about a third of it I guess, after which I had sandwiches and whiskey in the kitchen just like in the movies.

At the opposite end of the social scale from these genteel and refined goings-on were the large number of fall Foul Suppers I played at, as part of a concert-party, in country community halls. Here the fare was rough and roughly presented, but it was mountainous and excellent, and after a whole evening of tickling the ivories, as more than one round-faced farmer described it, the food was welcome. It was pure barter I guess—those with gifts served those who had the food. The only thing was that *tickling the ivories* was a euphemism for pressing untuned pianos into sound, pianos with keyboards from which all the tooth enamel had been removed, leaving only brown wooden stumps. Generally one was playing for audiences that considered Gilbert and Sullivan too highbrow.

Associated with this banquet circuit were numerous other times in the city when I was subjected to ridiculous embarrassment with untrained male voice ensembles, sing-songs, and other improvisatory traps—embarrassments usually connected with the absurd and pompous rituals of Canadian Babbittry. What was hardest to bear was the jollity, since what I felt was the correspondence between the hollowness of the proceedings and the hollowness of my nervous stomach.

Since I was very religious I was always getting involved, as a youthful penitent, in religious concerts and services to mankind. One such involvement was with an old codger who taught singing as a sideline and whose struggling pupils I accompanied. He always seemed to be excusing their public performances to me on physical grounds since he was a veterinarian, and a common excuse for the ladies was that this time they were not only having trouble with their time but with their periods. This particular Sunday, which was Christmas Day, he assembled all his pupils and their friends for a unique performance of Handel's *Messiah*, accompanied by piano, and when after several hours the blessed piece was apparently over, I retired to my room to have an appropriately symbolic dinner of a loaf of bread and a can of sardines.

PATRICK FRIESEN

from *The Shunning*

he had disobeyed. had waded barefoot in the creek before the weather was warm enough. you could easy have got a cold she said. she brought out a spool of #10 thread and tied his ankle to a tree with a 5 foot length.

break that and you get strapping.

mother hoeing

her red arms
her eight-month belly
her hair tied into a knot

then the bright hoe raised high
slashing down like a sun
again   again
and mother stoops to pick up the mangled snake
slings it over the fence   a yellow rope

she wipes her hands on her apron
nostrils wrinkling she turns to me   smell this
I inhale the musk and grease of her hands

. . . .

I latch the barn door
bend to pick up a pail of milk
then wobble through snowdrifts

a steel guitar cries from our house
I pause   the night below zero
and listen to Peter's nasal song

He lifted me up to a heavenly place

I look up   there
icy sheets of northern lights
planets reeling above the barn

only words sung   the guitar
encounter this star-marred night
and utter folly

. . . .

rivers

a woman sags in ropes
her hair seaweed

where horses ford
bridle and sword glinting

the river grandfather swims
naked in his slim strength

where mosquitoes cloud a paddlewheeler

these rivers flowing me back
and   as in a dream   I cross and cross

I kiss His hands His feet
and though my lips redden
I cannot taste His blood

to find love

to find love
I sit on the stone between tomb
and Christ risen   pale with hunger

to find Jesus   alone   in the garden
before the serpent crawls through the fence

. . . .

a silver fall   water
fall arcing   aching
cock crow

singing the hollow

hallow
the hollow   singing

still
in that cold face
singing yes   yes   yes
singing   still
at cock crow
at caught cock crow
in the face of

no god
know

. . . .

the crouped child choking
and mother holding him over a steaming kettle

the child sprawled on gravel   licking his blood

the child   rolling his pantlegs to the knees
wading down twin creek   cattails bowing
this boy   his feet and calves mud-smeared
is man here   the caught corpse

one hand in water
one boot off   the other untied
his white foot nudging the rifle stock

his temple   a blue hole the bullet made

....

now his narrow home
a mound   a stone

wild rose bushes
barbed wire
and headstones on the other side

Franz Reimer
Katharina Plett
Bernhard Dyck

until the trumpet
until morning cracks open his grave
he lies apart
his face to the sun going down red

a part of them   Peter
who wanted so much what wasn't

if love could clothe his bones in flesh

terrain

in thrall to the roots,
perennial in their mode,
I find the constant windflower
easily abandoning its petals.

this land is daubed with ashen easters,
with blue-eyed grass and goldenrod.

there is something vague in the colour,
something explicit in the form.

fire-confirmed and tree-broken,
this land holds the valerian edible
along the railroad, along the marsh;
the birdsfoot violet in the churchyard.

and yes, in thrall to the oak
and all divining months
when I hardened in grandfather's desert
of thistle, stone and snakeroot.

wings

trees have taken on flesh

leaves curl around each last sound
and hold them unheard
until they fall to earth

(how could that whispering giant
dropping in the dark
hold such a clamour   such surprise)

the bone field is littered with the machine
and clothes once worn by angels

ragweed prevails
though hewn here and there by wings

the rain has softened
over the husk of a broken world
amid the blue sizzle of blue fires and mist
fall's turning breathes

leaves draw blood   dropping
they release silence
like smoke in the purple weed

sunday afternoon

on sunday afternoons all the fathers in town slept
I think they dreamed of old days and death
sometimes you could hear them cry
the summer air was still at the window
flies on the screen and the radio playing softly in the kitchen

mother slid a fresh matrimonial cake onto potholders on the
    stove
picked up a book a true book of someone else's life
sunglasses a pitcher of lemonade and a straw hat
spread a blue blanket in the backyard near the lilac shrubs for
    shade
lay down one ear hearing children in the garden
she never escaped all the way nor did she want to not quite
this much on a sunday afternoon went a long way

downtown boys rode main street toward fiery crashes they
    imagined
twisted wrecks with radios playing
rock 'n' roll insulting the highway
townspeople gathered on the shoulder
standing as near as they could to the impossible moment
    between what's here and not

a girl's body sprawled in the ditch no one knew at first whose
    daughter she was
though someone pulled her skirt down for decency
the smell of alcohol and fuel everywhere
her lipstick so so red beneath the headlights
they couldn't take their eyes from her lips
what was she doing in a wild car like that? who was she?

at night I shivered in bed wondering how to get out of town
side-stepping wrecks they were everywhere on all the roads
    heading out toward the lights and laughter
a dented hubcap an amazing shoe with its laces still done up
    made you wonder how someone could step right out of a
    shoe like that like the flesh was willing or surprised
    or not there to begin with

in nightmares angry lords walked through my room
it took my breath away how ferocious love could be
sometimes jesus hung on the wall or was it the shadow of an
    elm?

in the morning at the kitchen table green tomatoes on the
    window sill we held devotions with careful hands
father's eyes focussed hard on me so he wouldn't remember
    but of course he did
listening often to mother's sunny childhood dreams
I thought I was free I was a child with a dancing mother
and my town was filled with children and my town had
    backstreets and sheds and black dogs and sugar trees
    but she disappeared and he died and I got out I'm getting
    out I'm getting out
what I left there the child gathering raspberries in an enamel
    bowl
he's not dead he went back to where you are before you're
    born again
waiting for the next time and another town

dream of the black river

I'm dreaming a dream of the black river where I can't swim
    I'm dreaming my last breath I'm dreaming how things
    are almost over I'm dreaming a possible swimmer with
    powerful arms to hold me
the river is cruel and cold I would drown for warmth
my legs dangle beneath me in the water my hands perform
    circles my lips are open for a kiss who will kiss them?

a figure on shore I can make it out someone knows I'm out
    here someone appears poised on a rock a diver about to
    thread evening air and enter this dark water
but no one moves there is only a pose of intention and
    nothing happens ever again

my darling lord take me all the way my fishtailing body my
hearing my faithful tongue
show me early morning first light across yellow fields could
crack my heart
I had eyes enough to see it all blue eyes that didn't care except
to see and see and see
I stood in the long grass and turned around and around it was
all there all the love its earth and flight and the rain at
night
move me again my darling I used to unlace my shoes and go
barefoot I walked through grass felt the earthworm's
trembling tunnel sometimes I was so light I walked above
ground it made me laugh my legs streaming with power or
light I could see it shining in my veins I was a snake
sloughing his life with no hope for another there was
nothing to want or need or do there was nothing

nothing feels like something when you straddle a bough high
in the sugar tree or ma's singing in the kitchen
when you love someone feels so light you could walk without
shoes anywhere you could doff your hat and fly

my love take me away all the way to where my lies are true
take me beneath your umbrella of water that will be good
enough for me to stand in the rain dreaming the dreams
of the dead and living dogs barking in backyards
remembering the love and terror that brought me here
my beauty lay me down and take me all the way I'm dreaming
the dream of my death or someone is it doesn't feel like
me anymore
he's gasping the river is in his ears he's banging at the
window he wants to break into the swimmer's dream he
wants another another

KEITH LOUISE FULTON

there is no special structure women have

you say you just want to be normal again

the pregnancy is almost full term
the baby is pressing tiny hips against your ribs
the head has dropped
into your pelvis
your bones are structured for this work
they carry the weight of this
new life and your own
in balance

like you I longed
in the heaviest month for
the asymmetry of the normal
that I remembered as light motion
without much consequence

yet even with that last month
seven years past
these sons and daughter
people my dreams and press heavy
against the ribs of my mind and still deeper down
on the girl's light-boned
swift flight into a possible sky

there is no special structure women have
for the work of loving children
every minute all our lives

we balance the unimpregnable past against
a future we fear to imagine
and carry on
ignorant of our delivery

this way of labour
we allow ourselves
you and I
to call normal

KRISTJANA GUNNARS

From Memory I

(at most i've heard of 25
infants born to a woman
none of them twins
5 to 15 is average
2 to 4 might live

you expect them to die
you want them to die
food is scarce, life
is better where god is)

400 of us leave on the verona
wednesday july 12
from seydisfjördur, gudrídur
pregnant with a son
to cut trees in canada

(makes sure it's a son;
lay on her right side
during conception; pisses
into a washbasin under the moon
puts a needle in the bottom

next morning: it's rusty, all's
well)
halldór briem interprets for us

son of eggert briem of skagafjördur
all the way to granton
july 16

(gudrídur is larger
on the right side, her right breast
is bigger: it's a boy)
for sure

leave granton by train
sunday to glascow, 4 days
later leave glascow at 12
thursday july 20

the trip goes well over the sea
the keel below is rusty
the east coast of canada grows
in the north, halldór briem

says it's virgin forest
all of it, says

they want more settlers
they call it
god's country

From Memory II

you want to know the trick of fertility
want to know the trick of infertility
to know how to stay together
know if the other is faithful

i'm forgetting fast
it's a long trip from glascow to quebec
this is the last story i'll tell

(hannes hannesson, scaleeye
turned 70 in 1885, told 3 stories
every night between february 2
& may 12 & still had more to tell)

the place is bottomless with stories
from glascow to quebec
you want to know about dusksleep days
when men lumbered in, threw off
their snowgear, put on the nightshoes
& sat down to knit, the women

sat down to knit too
(it's a long yarn) the best way

to stay together: don't air your quilt
on sundays, don't give each other
a sharp tool

eat the heart of a ptarmigan
put two tongues under your tongue & kiss
hang a raven's heart around your neck
hang a crow's heart around your neck

the best way
to test faithfulness: put
a magnet under her pillow at night
if she's true, she'll turn over & embrace you
if not, she'll turn over the other way
& fall with a crash on the floor
(or he will)

this is the last story i'll tell
the best way to become fertile: drink
mare's milk, dry a fox's testicle
in the shade, stir in wine, drink
after menstruation, or

(this is the only time i'll tell you)
during love, lie
with the hips above the shoulders
the best way

to avoid fertility: cut open your shin
put in a bit of mercury & heal over

there's more
i may tell you more, provided
you give me a long life in canada

From Memory XII

i begin to think the country
from quebec to winnipeg is based
on the pitfall principle
simple (but effective) traps

a container in the ground
a shallow water basin, a dis-
assembled box weighted
down with rock

an artificial fly, when i leap
the earth turns to water
a barrel sinks in the lake
raw meat lies on a ramp

wherever i look, spikes
stand ready to drive in
to my head, clip off my hand

a trench splits the road
especially on rainy nights
everything fills with water

unnecessary graveyards, all
the children complain about them
severe stomach pain
suffocation, insects in the mouth

3 days, august 14 to 17
on the steamboat to winnipeg
the drinking water is pure
poison by now, full

of creatures fallen in

Stefán Eyjólfsson XV

i've jotted my notes in the corner
of the newsprint sigtryggur
brought from reykjavík, paper
soiled now with offal

our first battle, first winter
is past: every third man
rolled up, burned or buried
it's a long trip we're taking

we bleed freely like freshly
killed birds, now we lie
for a short time, coagulate
the blood on our feathers

i've learned to leave it at that
the bird, to plug the throat
with a ball of oilcloth, put
wads of string in the nostrils

when the blood continues to creep
out, the bird stiffens
very fast, a tap with the hammer
snaps the wingbones in two

once settled, on our backs
like this we can't fly again
we're mounted into the prairie
pinned by broken promise, by

confusion, each man thinks
for himself now, the feathers parted
with a barren strip, pinned
by the unwilling in winnipeg

who won't make the journey north
with food, our own people
cut off
in the middle of the breast

Jóhann Briem 2, II

hannes scheving (dead 1726)
has been unearthed
in the munkathverár-cemetery
inadvertently

jón farmer, curious
has them dig it all up
the coffin strung in black
tanned leather, nailed

tight around the gable-
end with brass tacks
one side of the gable-head
loose where the corpse is

slipped in
for a burial like that
i'd go to new iceland
(when you're poor you're buried

without graveclothes, without
coffin, tied to a thin board)
though it's slow sailing
i can't say

it's bad, this moving over
from old to new iceland
a bit crowded on the boats

& wagons, unusual
food, some stomach
illness, mainly
for the kids, but other-

wise i can't say
it's as bad as the great
smallpox of 1707
& 1786, or the famines

of 1756 & 1784 (with
starvation on every
farm, no one
had anything for any-

one) only
30 or 40 children are dead
of the stomach pain
going to canada (11

in the first group dead
on arrival in winnipeg)
but it's not as bad

as 1785 (when, without
timber, you were buried
without even a board, dumped
with everyone else together

under a cairn
in the black-tanned night
nailed in with brass
stars) not that

bad

A Long Production

the world of that which is big
continues to grow & distance
itself from us.   our devices
become more strange as we try to see

what is fixed, what moves
what follows sun

for this we have a mirror
reflecting a mirror, reflecting a mirror
reflecting into a spectrograph
atop Kitt Peak, Arizona

the makeup of sun, the parts
are coming down

we can find ourselves
reflected in that Diego Rivera
"Ford Production Line.   Body Presses and
Assembly of Automobile Chassis"

long name, big fresco
"brutal picture of factory mass production"
welding machines, flames in steel
it was always a hard reality

we have been working for a living
since day began, making things big &
seeing them
work

JAN HORNER

A Letter to My Mother

So this is my life
looking away to the trees
the rocket spires
now milked and cleansed
by the baby no longer inside
but whose drama I am now into
my little boy with his rights
and perfect teeth

Having left my son
I come to the coast to write another
to write as a mother
to remember your father
Writing, a guest life
inviting my own retirement
Morning wakes us to different excuses
flowers in the rooms
Writing, a terrible work if you can get it
all my versions
gone over the hill and home

The fear of my being alone
comforts us with truth
if we leave it long enough
if we leave it last and later
Mr. Wrong will become your father
You will understand his slippers
the old man shirts
the tea towel round his waist
as the reason your daughter still smokes
And that this is where
I've always been headed
to someone's son
your father, my lover
a woman worth her weight
in desire
that you should know
your loving child
you, her first lover, her first speaker
she will have courage
and will find once more
all those who cherish her
truly

MARY HORODYSKI

Housecraft

when i washed the floor
in my bedroom last thursday
and poured the grimy water
from the pail into the toilet
i watched the rag go down too
this alarmed me
so i phoned my mom
mom   i said   i was washing
my floor just now   and i guess
she knows what i'm like
because she said   you flushed
the rag down the toilet didn't you
quick   she said   put your hand in
and get it   i said   it was too late
so then she wanted to know
how big the rag was because
if it was the size of a
washcloth then it would go down
readily and this she knew
from experience and also diapers
will sometimes go down as women
know from experience from the time
there were cloth diapers but often
you can catch them in time but if you
can't then flush the toilet quick
before anyone uses it so that
if it backs up at least it's clean
water and if it doesn't back up
keep flushing and if you're lucky
you can send it down the street
and let someone else pay the plumber's
bill   so i did and it worked and now

when i walk down langside i look
for the roto-rooter out of the corner
of my eye so as not to attract
suspicion to myself but when i look
my mother in the eye i am proud
of women's secrets

At 7

At grandma's house in beausejour
we chase each other around
the double lot counting the
birdhouses grandpa makes   dipping
rhubarb in coffee mugs filled
with sugar   picking raspberries
fresh peas and tiny sweet carrots
grandma sends us all away
when she strangles chickens and
plucks the feathers from their skins
but later when we come back we
play with their feet pulling on
tendons to make the toes move

grandpa is a big man over 6 feet
tall   he doesn't have many teeth or
speak good english   we are scared
when he calls us to sit on his lap
when grandma washes clothes in
the kitchen with her wringer washer
she cries and tells my sisters that she
was scared of grandpa too   that fifteen
is too young for a girl to be married
to a man she doesn't know and sometimes

she says he had beat her   i am too
young to know but later they will
tell me and also they will point
out the shrine of our lady behind
the church that grandpa helped to build
when he dies at the hospital the priest
will come to grandma's house into the
living room and call her anna and though
i don't understand polish i see my grandma's
face go wrinkly with tears and i take my
baby sisters to wait outside by
the raspberry bushes for our mom to
come home to grandma's house   i will
want to go to prayers but they
will say i am too young but at
the funeral the priest will ask me
to carry the water and my sister to
carry the host and i will walk past
grandpa's coffin and be afraid
that he will reach for me and ask
me to sit on his lap   later in
winnipeg my parents will tell how
the birds sang at the cemetery to thank
grandpa for the birdhouses he built

three uncles will die by drowning
one my brother will bring to shore
behind the motorboat belonging to my
cousin   when my mother gets the phone call
from kenora the message will be garbled
and she won't know if her son
is dead also   and i will watch
her scrub the taps of the bathroom

sink with comet and a toothbrush as a
woman's ritual to ward away
death   she will also visit her
mother every day for a year in the geriatric
ward of st boniface hospital when
grandma has a stroke and i will go only
a few times but once i will see
grandma so mad she will spit her soup
across the room and my mother will be there
when she dies and when you go
to the health sciences centre i will ride
in the ambulance with you   with your
blood on my shoes and pants and will wait
all night awake because if i sleep
you might die and i will visit
you every day and for 3 nights i will
wash the walls and fridge and stove
and floors of your blood which has dried
and smells now of the same smell as
the chickens' blood in grandma's yard

my grandma had 10 children   my
mother had 7   and i will have
none   our children will remain locked
from our lives   one day when we
live together my aunt will give us this
same fridge of my grandma's i opened
this afternoon   and one evening we
will fight and you will try to
throw it at me and one night i will dream
of my grandpa and you will hold me
when i wake   and one day i will
ask you to marry me and you will refuse

and this i know when i am 7 years old
at grandma's house and i lie on my
stomach in the grass and fall asleep
while reading the book my mom brought
me and later on on fort street you will
tell me how when you were 7
you fell asleep while reading
in your room and you dreamt of a girl
dreaming and i will tell you how
children grow old

SMARO KAMBOURELI

from *in the second person*

Wednesday, December 21, 1980

I am going to start a journal today. I will begin entering, again, the labyrinth of the real. I will let light fall on the fragments I scattered in the Aegean. My reality is beyond my dreams. And my passport is just a notebook of motion signs. Each point of entry has more than one exit, some of them marked, others erased by sudden lightning.

I'm lost in the pages of my old journals. As I reread them, I catch myself playing hopscotch. My playmate shrinks behind the lines when I win. But when I stumble, I withdraw, smiling.

I am a silhouette dancing outside myself. I expose the splitting of my body. The braided minds. Intimacy interwoven with/out design.

February 6, 1981

My language.
My Greek rusty.
My awareness of making mistakes when I use English.
My language that tortures me every time I dare use it.
My language that refuses to flow from the pen onto the page.
My language locked within my body.
My astonishment when I realized I was dreaming in English.

I gaze at my Greek typewriter in despair. In shame.
Dust has settled on the keyboard. And I forget how
to type a question mark: is it a period above the line,
backspace, and then a comma under the period? or a colon,
backspace, and then a comma typed over the bottom period
of the colon? The difference is not only visual.

February 8, 1981

you treasure every dead moment
of your life. memory is the
saving grace of the emptiness
that fills you.

I want you to die.
Any form of death will do.

let me ask you then. i think
of aquin and suicide all the
time. is this an intellectual
exercise, a fallacious gesture,
or are you running, as usual,
ahead of me sounding the water?
do you know what i have to kill,
metaphorically speaking?

I'm no exception. I changed language, I grew a second skin, wrapped around my self another self. I've become a metonymy of my past. My image of myself these days is that of a fractured bone. A fractured bone that heals itself.

Blackout: "I am the anamorphosis
of my own death, and of boredom."

Banff/August 5, 1981

i made a bonfire out of my greek alphabet
faces flickered
bones rattled
voices trembled
familiar shapes shook
the flames
with dismay
at my hubris

it's an
act of
love i
whispered
as i
cuddled
myself
closer
to the
warmth
keeping
a safe
distance
it's an
act of love
you should
be grateful
when i
need a
place to die
i'll call
you back

ROBERT KROETSCH

Syllogisms of Desire

A. All dogs have fleas.

My bed and blankets all are rank
with itching; back, belly, bum and
balls all burn.

Therefore my dog has fleas but keeps
me scratching.

B. *Whosoeuer desireth to live vertuously,*
desireth to auoide fornication.

Whosoever desires the above
has never heard a Tristan grieve
for pale Iseult, has never wept
where sad Francesca and Paolo move:

nor dug an early grave,
nor drunk wine from a sieve.

C. Man is what he eats.

For breakfast, two raw eggs:
kidney for lunch, with turnip
and mushroom red in the peppered
juice of a crushed onion: fresh
nutmeg and gin at six, with pods
of vanilla oyster-crammed: neck
(after the ten o'clock news)
of mutton fried in deep hot
fat, two raw eggs, and one
small rhinoceros horn.

Ergo: come, sweet, I must
in thee abide.

D. All beauty lies in the beholder's eyes.

Radiant Apollo, god of sun
and wisdom, giver of song,
healer of mankind, teller
of past and future, right and wrong,
bringer of peace and harmony and good:
embraced the branches of a tree
and kissed the wood.

Therefore: you certainly shall want me yet
like Pasiphaë, hot for a big white bull,
trotting the pastures in a perfect sweat.

E. Socrates met Xantippe.

Did he ask: What
is justice? Did he
ask: Young lady, what
do you mean by love?
Did he unhook her
brassiere?

All men are mortal.

F. All women praise this poem.

These lines have taught
you all the difference between
Thou Shalt and Thou Shalt Not.

Therefore: now try our dialectic skill,
and let us one on other work our will.

Projected Visit

The crops are off
now, the harvest
done: in Alberta
even the sun is
bleached
by the shortening
day; the blackbirds,

lost in a prairie
graveyard, grieve
on a barbed wire
fence; the wind
walks in the night,
trying for unlocked
doors . . .

        But what if
the first snow falls:
if the partridge does not
chirr from the stubbled
field; if the fence
has not held; if my
great tall
        father
his eyes
        forgiving
an errant son
does not stoop
from the grave to
love me   home?

from *The Ledger*

a. "in bookkeeping, the book of final entry, in which a record of debits, credits, and all money transactions is kept."

the
book
of
columns

page 33: James Darling

1880

Mar 22: to sawing square timber	1.44		
June 21: to 1 round cedar bed	3.50		
June 21: to 1 jack shingles	.50		
Dec 4: to sawing mable [*sic*]	1.50	Nov 4/82 by logs	4.10

(it doesn't balance)

some pages torn out (
by accident)
some pages remaining (
by accident)

page 62: Nicholas Neubecker

1893

Nov 16: to chopping 8 bags	.40
Dec 19: to chopping 880 lbs	.49
: to elm scantling	.18

the poet: by accident
finding in the torn ledger

(IT DOESN'T BALANCE)

the green poem:

my grandfather, Henry (dead)
in his watermill (gone)
on the Teeswater River,
on the road between Formosa and
Belmore, needing a new ledger:

the ledger itself (surviving)
purchased in the Bruce County
Drug and Book Store (Price:
$1.00 PAID), the leather cover
brown. In gold: *THE LEDGER:*

EVERYTHING I WRITE
I SAID, IS A SEARCH
(is debit, is credit)

is a search

for some pages

remaining

(by accident)

the poet: finding
in the torn ledger

the column straight
the column broken

FINDING

everything you write
my wife, my daughters, said
is a search for the dead

the book of final entry
in which a record is kept.

b. "a horizontal piece of timber secured to the uprights supporting the putlogs in a scaffolding, or the like."

The Canada Gazette, August 17, 1854:
"Notice is hereby given that the undermentioned lands . . . in the County of Bruce, U.C., will be open for sale to actual settlers . . . The price to be Ten shillings per acre . . . Actual occupation to be immediate and continuous . . ."

To raise a barn;

cut down a forest.

To raise oats and hay;

burn the soil.

To raise cattle and hogs;

kill the bear
kill the mink
kill the marten
kill the lynx
kill the fisher
kill the beaver
kill the moose

"As to the climate of the district, Father Holzer cannot praise it enough. He declares that during the first nine months of his residence here they had only one funeral, and that was of a man 84 years old."

A Pristine Forest
A Pristine Forest

"That winter, therefore, timbers of elm and maple and pine were cut the necessary lengths, hewed and dressed and hauled by means of the oxen to the barn site. Cedar logs were sawn in suitable lengths and shingles split from these blocks . . ."

"TO THE SAUGEEN!"
was the cry that spread.

Henry, the elder of the two brothers, was born in 1856, across the river from the mill in a log shanty measuring (as specified in *The Canada Gazette*, August 17, 1854) at least sixteen feet by eighteen.

Shaping the trees
into logs (burn
the slash) into
timbers and planks.

Shaping the trees
into ledgers.
Raising the barn.

That they might sit down
a forest had fallen.

to a pitcher of Formosa beer

Shaping the trees.
Into shingles.
Into scantling.
Into tables and chairs.

Have a seat, John.
Sit down, Henry.

That they might sit down
a forest/had fallen.

page 119: John O. Miller, brickmaker in Mildmay

1888

Aug 17: to cedar shingles	12.50	Aug 17: by Brick 2500 at 50¢	12.50

(I'll be damned. It balances.)

yes:no
no:yes

"...a specimen of the self-made men who have made Canada what it is, and of which no section has brought forth more or better representatives than the County of Bruce. Mr. Miller was never an office-seeker, but devoted himself strictly and energetically to the pursuit of his private business, and on his death was the owner of a very large and valuable property..."

Shaping the trees.
Pushing up daisies.

Have another glass, John.
Ja, ja. What the hell.

What's the matter, John?
My bones ache.

Take a day off, John.
No time.

A horizontal piece of timber
supporting the putlogs
in a scaffolding, or the like.

(specimens of the self-made
men who have made Canada
what it is)

The barn is still standing
(the mill, however, is gone)
sound as the day it was raised.

No time.
August 17, 1888.

No time.

Shaping the trees.
Pushing up daisies.

I'll be damned.
It balances.

MARGARET LAURENCE

The Mask of the Bear

In winter my Grandfather Connor used to wear an enormous coat made out of the pelt of a bear. So shaggy and coarse-furred was this coat, so unevenly coloured in patches ranging from amber to near-black, and so vile-smelling when it had become wet with snow, that it seemed to have belonged when it was alive to some lonely and giant Kodiak crankily roaming a high frozen plateau, or an ancient grizzly scarred with battles in the sinister forests of the north. In actuality, it had been an ordinary brown bear and it had come, sad to say, from no more fabled a place than Galloping Mountain, only a hundred miles from Manawaka. The skin had once been given to my grandfather as payment, in the days when he was a blacksmith, before he became a hardware merchant and developed the policy of cash only. He had had it cobbled into a coat by the local shoemaker, and Grandmother Connor had managed to sew in the lining. How long ago that was, no one could say for sure, but my mother, the eldest of his family, said she could not remember a time when he had not worn it. To me, at the age of ten and a half, this meant it must be about a century old. The coat was so heavy that I could not even lift it by myself. I never used to wonder how he could carry that phenomenal weight on himself or why he would choose to, because it was obvious that although he was old he was still an extraordinarily strong man, built to shoulder weights.

Whenever I went into Simlow's Ladies' Wear with my mother, and made grotesque faces at myself in the long mirror while she tried on dresses, Millie Christopherson who worked there would croon a phrase which made me break into snickering until my mother, who was death on bad manners, tapped anxiously at my shoulders with her slender, nervous hands. *It's you, Mrs. MacLeod,* Millie would say feelingly, *no kidding it's absolutely you.* I appropriated the phrase for my grandfather's winter coat. *It's you,* I would simper nastily at him, although never, of course, aloud.

In my head I sometimes called him "The Great Bear." The name had many associations other than his coat and his surliness. It was the way he would stalk around the Brick House as though it were a cage, on Sundays, impatient for the new week's beginning that would release him into the only freedom he knew, the acts of work. It was the way he would take to the basement whenever a man came to call upon Aunt Edna, which in those days was not often, because—as I had overheard my mother outlining in sighs to my father—most of the single men her age in Manawaka considered that the time she had spent working in Winnipeg had made more difference than it really had, and the situation wasn't helped by her flyaway manner (whatever that might mean). But if ever she was asked out to a movie, and the man was waiting and making stilted weather-chat with Grandmother Connor, Grandfather would prowl through the living room as though seeking a place of rest and not finding it, would stare fixedly without speaking, and would then descend the basement steps to the rocking chair which sat beside the furnace. Above ground, he would not have been found dead sitting in a rocking chair, which he considered a piece of furniture suitable only for the elderly, of whom he was never in his own eyes one. From his cave, however, the angry crunching of the wooden rockers against the cement floor would reverberate throughout the house, a kind of sub-verbal Esperanto, a disapproval which even the most obtuse person could not fail to comprehend.

In some unformulated way, I also associated the secret name with Great Bear Lake, which I had seen only on maps and which I imagined to be a deep vastness of black water, lying somewhere very far beyond our known prairies of tamed fields and barbed-wire fences, somewhere in the regions of jagged rock and eternal ice, where human voices would be drawn into a cold and shadowed stillness without leaving even a trace of warmth.

One Saturday afternoon in January, I was at the rink when my grandfather appeared unexpectedly. He was wearing his formidable coat, and to say he looked out of place among the skaters thronging around the edges of the ice would be putting it mildly. Embarrassed, I whizzed over to him.

"There you are, Vanessa—about time," he said, as though he had been searching for me for hours. "Get your skates off now, and come along. You're to come home with me for supper. You'll be staying the night at our place. Your dad's gone away out to Freehold, and your mother's gone with him. Fine time to pick for it. It's blowing up for a blizzard, if you ask me. They'll not get back for a couple of days, more than likely. Don't see why he don't just tell people to make their own way in to the hospital. Ewen's too easy-going. He'll not get a penny nor a word of thanks for it, you can bet your life on that."

My father and Dr. Cates used to take the country calls in turn. Often when my father went out in the winter, my mother would go with him, in case the old Nash got stuck in the snow and also to talk and thus prevent my father from going to sleep at the wheel, for falling snow has a hypnotic effect.

"What about Roddie?" I asked, for my brother was only a few months old.

"The old lady's keeping care of him," Grandfather Connor replied abruptly.

The old lady meant my Grandmother MacLeod, who was actually a few years younger than Grandfather Connor. He always referred to her in this way, however, as a calculated insult, and here my sympathies were with him for once. He maintained, quite correctly, that she gave herself airs because her husband had been a doctor and now her son was one, and that she looked down on the Connors because they had come from famine Irish (although at least, thank God, Protestant). The two of them seldom met, except at Christmas, and never exchanged more than a few words. If they had ever really clashed it would have been like a brontosaurus running headlong into a tyrannosaurus.

"Hurry along now," he said, when I had taken off my skates and put on my snow boots. "You've got to learn not to dawdle. You're an awful dawdler, Vanessa."

I did not reply. Instead, when we left the rink I began to take exaggeratedly long strides. But he paid no attention to my attempt to reproach him with my speed. He walked beside me steadily and silently, wrapped in his great fur coat and his authority.

The Brick House was at the other end of town, so while I shuffled through the snow and pulled my navy wool scarf up around my nose against the steel cutting edge of the wind, I thought about the story I was setting down in a five-cent scribbler at nights in my room. I was much occupied by the themes of love and death, although my experience of both had so far been gained principally from the Bible, which I read in the same way as I read Eaton's Catalogue or the collected works of Rudyard Kipling—because I had to read something, and the family's finances in the thirties did not permit the purchase of enough volumes of *Doctor Doolittle* or the *Oz* books to keep me going.

For the love scenes, I gained useful material from The Song of Solomon. *Let him kiss me with the kisses of his mouth, for thy love is better than wine*, or *By night on my bed I sought him whom my soul loveth; I sought him but I found him not.* My interpretation was somewhat vague, and I was not helped to any appreciable extent by the explanatory bits in small print at the beginning of each chapter—*The church's love unto Christ. The church's fight and victory in temptation*, et cetera. These explanations did not puzzle me, though, for I assumed even then that they had simply been put there for the benefit of gentle and unworldly people such as my Grandmother Connor, so that they could read the Holy Writ without becoming upset. To me, the woman in The Song was some barbaric queen, beautiful and terrible, and I could imagine her, wearing a long robe of leopard skin and one or two heavy gold bracelets, pacing an alabaster courtyard and keening her unrequited love.

The heroine in my story (which took place in ancient Egypt—my ignorance of this era did not trouble me) was very like the woman in The Song of Solomon, except that mine had long wavy auburn hair, and when her beloved left her, the only thing she could bring herself to eat was an avocado, which seemed to me considerably more stylish and exotic than apples in lieu of love. Her young man was a gifted carver, who had been sent out into the desert by the cruel pharaoh (pharaohs were always cruel—of this I was positive) in order to carve a giant sphinx for the royal tomb. Should I have her die while he was away? Or would it be better if he perished out in the desert? Which of them did I like the least? With the characters whom I liked best, things always turned out right in the end. Yet the death scenes had an undeniable appeal, a sombre splendour, with (as it said in Ecclesiastes) the mourners going about the streets and all the daughters of music brought low. Both death and love seemed regrettably far from Manawaka and the snow, and my grandfather stamping his feet on the front porch of the Brick House and telling me to do the same or I'd be tracking the wet in all over the hardwood floor.

The house was too warm, almost stifling. Grandfather burned mainly birch in the furnace, although it cost twice as much as poplar, and now that he had retired from the hardware store, the furnace gave him something to do and so he was forever stoking it. Grandmother Connor was in the dining room, her stout body in its brown rayon dress bending over the canary's cage.

"Hello, pet," she greeted me. "You should have heard Birdie just a minute ago—one of those real long trills. He's been moulting lately, and this is the first time he's sung in weeks."

"Gee," I said enthusiastically, for although I was not fond of canaries, I was extremely fond of my grandmother. "That's swell. Maybe he'll do it again."

"Messy things, them birds," my grandfather commented. "I can never see what you see in a fool thing like that, Agnes."

My grandmother did not attempt to reply to this.

"Would you like a cup of tea, Timothy?" she asked.

"Nearly supper-time, ain't it?"

"Well, not for a little while yet."

"It's away past five," my grandfather said. "What's Edna been doing with herself?"

"She's got the pot-roast in," my grandmother answered, "but it's not done yet."

"You'd think a person could get a meal on time," he said, "considering she's got precious little else to do."

I felt, as so often in the Brick House, that my lungs were in danger of exploding, that the pressure of silence would become too great to be borne. I wanted to point out, as I knew Grandmother Connor would never do, that it wasn't Aunt Edna's fault there were no jobs anywhere these days, and that, as my mother often said of her, she worked her fingers to the bone here so she wouldn't need to feel beholden to him for her keep, and that they would have had to get a hired girl if she hadn't been here, because Grandmother Connor couldn't look after a place this size any more. Also, that the dining-room clock said precisely ten minutes past five, and the evening meal in the Connor house was always at six o'clock on the dot. And—and—a thousand other arguments rose up and nearly choked me. But I did not say anything. I was not that stupid. Instead, I went out to the kitchen.

Aunt Edna was wearing her coral sweater and grey pleated skirt, and I thought she looked lovely, even with her apron on. I always thought she looked lovely, though, whatever she was wearing, but if ever I told her so, she would only laugh and say it was lucky she had a cheering section of one.

"Hello, kiddo," she said. "Do you want to sleep in my room tonight, or shall I make up the bed in the spare room?"

"In your room," I said quickly, for this meant she would let me try out her lipstick and use some of her Jergens hand-lotion, and if I could stay awake until she came to bed, we would whisper after the light was out.

"How's *The Pillars of the Nation* coming along?" she asked.

That had been my epic on pioneer life. I had proceeded to the point in the story where the husband, coming back to the cabin one evening, discovered to his surprise that he was going to become a father. The way he ascertained this interesting fact was that he found his wife constructing a birch-bark cradle. Then came the discovery that Grandfather Connor had been a pioneer, and the story had lost its interest for me. If pioneers were like *that,* I had thought, my pen would be better employed elsewhere.

"I quit that one," I replied laconically. "I'm making up another—it's miles better. It's called *The Silver Sphinx*. I'll bet you can't guess what it's about."

"The desert? Buried treasure? Murder mystery?"

I shook my head.

"Love," I said.

"Good Glory," Aunt Edna said, straight-faced. "That sounds fascinating. Where do you get your ideas, Vanessa?"

I could not bring myself to say the Bible. I was afraid she might think this sounded funny.

"Oh, here and there," I replied noncommittally. "You know."

She gave me an inquisitive glance, as though she meant to question me further, but just then the telephone rang, and I rushed to answer it, thinking it might be my mother or father phoning from Freehold. But it wasn't. It was a voice I didn't know, a man's.

"Is Edna Connor there?"

"Just a minute, please," I cupped one hand over the mouthpiece fixed on the wall, and the other over the receiver.

"For you," I hissed, grinning at her. "A strange man!"

"Mercy," Aunt Edna said ironically, "these hordes of admirers will be the death of me yet. Probably Todd Jeffries from Burns' Electric about that busted lamp."

Nevertheless, she hurried over. Then, as she listened, her face became startled, and something else which I could not fathom.

"Heavens, where are you?" she cried at last. "At the station *here?* Oh Lord. Why didn't you write to say you were—well, sure I am, but—oh, never mind. No, you wait there. I'll come and meet you. You'd never find the house—"

I had never heard her talk this way before, rattlingly. Finally she hung up. Her face looked like a stranger's, and for some reason this hurt me.

"It's Jimmy Lorimer," she said. "He's at the C.P.R. station. He's coming here. Oh my God, I wish Beth were here."

"Why?" I wished my mother were here, too, but I could not see what difference it made to Aunt Edna. I knew who Jimmy Lorimer was. He was a man Aunt Edna had gone around with when she was in Winnipeg. He had given her the Attar of Roses in an atomiser bottle with a green net-covered bulb—the scent she always sprayed around her room after she had had a cigarette there. Jimmy Lorimer had been invested with a remote glamour in my imagination, but all at once I felt I was going to hate him.

I realised that Aunt Edna was referring to what Grandfather Connor might do or say, and instantly I was ashamed for having felt churlishly disposed towards Jimmy Lorimer. Even if he was a cad, a heel, or a nitwit, I swore I would welcome him. I visualised him as having a flashy appearance, like a riverboat gambler in a movie I had seen once, a checkered suit, a slender oiled moustache, a diamond tie-pin, a dangerous leer. Never mind. Never mind if he was Lucifer himself.

"I'm glad he's coming," I said staunchly.

Aunt Edna looked at me queerly, her mouth wavering as though she were about to smile. Then, quickly, she bent and hugged me, and I could feel her trembling. At this moment, Grandmother Connor came into the kitchen.

"You all right, pet?" she asked Aunt Edna. "Nothing's the matter, is it?"

"Mother, that was an old friend of mine on the phone just now. Jimmy Lorimer. He's from Winnipeg. He's passing through Manawaka. Is it all right if he comes here for dinner?"

"Well, of course, dear," Grandmother said. "What a lucky thing we're having the pot-roast. There's plenty. Vanessa, pet, you run down to the fruit cellar and bring up a jar of strawberries, will you? Oh, and a small jar of chili sauce. No, maybe the sweet mustard pickle would go better with the pot-roast. What do you think, Edna?"

She spoke as though this were the only important issue in the whole situation. But all the time her eyes were on Aunt Edna's face.

"Edna—" she said, with great effort, "is he—is he a good man, Edna?"

Aunt Edna blinked and looked confused, as though she had been spoken to in some foreign language.

"Yes," she replied.

"You're sure, pet?"

"Yes," Aunt Edna repeated, a little more emphatically than before.

Grandmother Connor nodded, smiled reassuringly, and patted Aunt Edna lightly on the wrist.

"Well, that's fine, dear. I'll just tell Father. Everything will be all right, so don't you worry about a thing."

When Grandmother had gone back to the living room, Aunt Edna began pulling on her black fur-topped overshoes. When she spoke, I didn't know whether it was to me or not.

"I didn't tell her a damn thing," she said in a surprised tone. "I wonder how she knows, or if she really does? *Good.* What a word. I wish I didn't know what she means when she says that. Or else that she knew what I mean when I say it. Glory, I wish Beth were here."

I understood then that she was not speaking to me, and that what she had to say could not be spoken to me. I felt chilled by my childhood, unable to touch her because of the freezing burden of my inexperience. I was about to say something, anything, however mistaken, when my aunt said *Sh*, and we both listened to the talk from the living room.

"A friend of Edna's is coming for dinner, Timothy," Grandmother was saying quietly. "A young man from Winnipeg."

A silence. Then, "Winnipeg!" my grandfather exclaimed, making it sound as though Jimmy Lorimer were coming here straight from his harem in Casablanca.

"What's he do?" Grandfather demanded next.

"Edna didn't say."

"I'm not surprised," Grandfather said darkly. "Well, I won't have her running around with that sort of fellow. She's got no more sense than a sparrow."

"She's twenty-eight," Grandmother said, almost apologetically. "Anyway, this is just a friend."

"Friend!" my grandfather said, annihilating the word. Then, not loudly, but with an odd vehemence, "you don't know a blame thing about men, Agnes. You never have."

Even I could think of several well-placed replies that my grandmother might have made, but she did not do so. She did not say anything. I looked at Aunt Edna, and saw that she had closed her eyes the way people do when they have a headache. Then we heard Grandmother's voice, speaking at last, not in her usual placid and unruffled way, but hesitantly.

"Timothy—please. Be nice to him. For my sake."

For my sake. This was so unlike my grandmother that I was stunned. She was not a person who begged you to be kind for her sake, or even for God's sake. If you were kind, in my grandmother's view, it was for its own sake, and the judgement of whether you had done well or not was up to the Almighty. *Judge not, that ye be not judged*—this was her favourite admonition to me when I lost my temper with one of my friends. As a devout Baptist, she believed it was a sin to pray for anything for yourself. You ought to pray only for strength to bear whatever the Lord saw fit to send you, she thought. I was never able to follow this advice, for although I would often feel a sense of uneasiness over the tone of my prayers, I was the kind of person who prayed frantically—"Please, God, please, please *please* let Ross MacVey like me better than Mavis." Grandmother Connor was not self-effacing in her lack of demands either upon God or upon her family. She merely believed that what happened to a person in this life was in Other Hands. Acceptance was at the heart of her. I don't think in her own eyes she ever lived in a state of bondage. To the rest of the family, thrashing furiously and uselessly in various snarled dilemmas, she must often have appeared to live in a state of perpetual grace, but I am certain she didn't think of it that way, either.

Grandfather Connor did not seem to have heard her.

"We won't get our dinner until all hours, I daresay," he said.

But we got our dinner as soon as Aunt Edna had arrived back with Jimmy Lorimer, for she flew immediately out to the kitchen and before we knew it we were all sitting at the big circular table in the dining room.

Jimmy Lorimer was not at all what I had expected. Far from looking like a Mississippi gambler, he looked just like anybody else, any uncle or grown-up cousin, unexceptional in every way. He was neither overwhelmingly handsome nor interestingly ugly. He was okay to look at, but as I said to myself, feeling at the same time a twinge of betrayal towards Aunt Edna, he was nothing to write home about. He wore a brown suit and a green tie. The only thing about him which struck fire was that he had a joking manner similar to Aunt Edna's, but whereas I felt at ease with this quality in her, I could never feel comfortable with the laughter of strangers, being uncertain where an including laughter stopped and taunting began.

"You're from Winnipeg, eh?" Grandfather Connor began. "Well, I guess you fellows don't put much store in a town like Manawaka."

Without waiting for affirmation or denial of this sentiment, he continued in an unbroken line.

"I got no patience with these people who think a small town is just nothing. You take a city, now. You could live in one of them places for twenty years, and you'd not get to know your next-door neighbour. Trouble comes along—who's going to give you a hand? Not a blamed soul."

Grandfather Connor had never in his life lived in a city, so his first-hand knowledge of their ways was, to say the least, limited. As for trouble—the thought of my grandfather asking any soul in Manawaka to give aid and support to him in any way whatsoever was inconceivable. He would have died of starvation, physical or spiritual, rather than put himself in any man's debt by so much as a dime or a word.

"Hey, hold on a minute," Jimmy Lorimer protested. "I never said that about small towns. As a matter of fact, I grew up in one myself. I came from McConnell's Landing. Ever heard of it?"

"I heard of it all right," Grandfather said brusquely, and no one could have told from his tone whether McConnell's Landing was a place of ill-repute or whether he simply felt his knowledge of geography was being doubted. "Why'd you leave, then?"

Jimmy shrugged. "Not much opportunity there. Had to seek my fortune, you know. Can't say I've found it, but I'm still looking."

"Oh, you'll be a tycoon yet, no doubt," Aunt Edna put in.

"You bet your life, kiddo," Jimmy replied. "You wait. Times'll change."

I didn't like to hear him say "kiddo." It was Aunt Edna's word, the one she called me by. It didn't belong to him.

"Mercy, they can't change fast enough for me," Aunt Edna said. "I guess I haven't got your optimism, though."

"Well, I haven't got it, either," he said, laughing, "but keep it under your hat, eh?"

Grandfather Connor had listened to this exchange with some impatience. Now he turned to Jimmy once more.

"What's your line of work?"

"I'm with Reliable Loan Company right now, Mr. Connor, but I don't aim to stay there permanently. I'd like to have my own business. Cars are what I'm really interested in. But it's not so easy to start up these days."

Grandfather Connor's normal opinions on social issues possessed such a high degree of clarity and were so frequently stated that they were well known even to me—all labour unions were composed of thugs and crooks; if people were unemployed it was due to their own laziness; if people were broke it was because they were not thrifty. Now, however, a look of intense and brooding sorrow came into his face, as he became all at once the champion of the poor and oppressed.

"Loan Company!" he said. "Them blood-suckers. They

wouldn't pay no mind to how hard-up a man might be. Take everything he has, without batting an eye. By the Lord Harry, I never thought the day would come when I'd sit down to a meal alongside one of them fellows."

Aunt Edna's face was rigid.

"Jimmy," she said. "Ignore him."

Grandfather turned on her, and they stared at one another with a kind of inexpressible rage but neither of them spoke. I could not help feeling sorry for Jimmy Lorimer, who mumbled something about his train leaving and began eating hurriedly. Grandfather rose to his feet.

"I've had enough," he said.

"Don't you want your dessert, Timothy?" Grandmother asked, as though it never occurred to her that he could be referring to anything other than the meal. It was only then that I realised that this was the first time she had spoken since we sat down at the table. Grandfather did not reply. He went down to the basement. Predictably, in a moment we could hear the wooden rockers of his chair thudding like retreating thunder. After dinner, Grandmother sat in the living room, but she did not get out the red cardigan she was knitting for me. She sat without doing anything, quite still, her hands folded in her lap.

"I'll let you off the dishes tonight, honey," Aunt Edna said to me. "Jimmy will help with them. You can try out my lipstick, if you like, only for Pete's sake wash it off before you come down again."

I went upstairs, but I did not go to Aunt Edna's room. I went into the back bedroom to one of my listening posts. In the floor there was a round hole which had once been used for a stove-pipe leading up from the kitchen. Now it was covered with a piece of brown-painted tin full of small perforations which had apparently been noticed only by me.

"Where does he get his lines, Edna?" Jimmy was saying. "He's like old-time melodrama."

"Yeh, I know." Aunt Edna sounded annoyed. "But let me say it, eh?"

"Sorry. Honest. Listen, can't you even—"

Scuffling sounds, then my aunt's nervous whisper.

"Not here, Jimmy. Please. You don't understand what they're—"

"I understand, all right. Why in God's name do you stay, Edna? Aren't you ever coming back? That's what I want to know."

"With no job? Don't make me laugh."

"I could help out, at first anyway—"

"Jimmy, don't talk like a lunatic. Do you really think I could?"

"Oh hell, I suppose not. Well, look at it this way. What if I wasn't cut out for the unattached life after all? What if the old leopard actually changed his spots, kiddo? What would you say to that?"

A pause, as though Aunt Edna were mulling over his words.

"That'll be the day," she replied. "I'll believe it when I see it."

"Well, Jesus, lady," he said, "I'm not getting down on my knees. Tell me one thing, though—don't you miss me at all? Don't you miss—everything? C'mon now—don't you? Not even a little bit?"

Another pause. She could not seem to make up her mind how to respond to the teasing quality of his voice.

"Yeh, I lie awake nights," she said at last, sarcastically.

He laughed. "Same old Edna. Want me to tell you something, kiddo? I think you're scared."

"Scared?" she said scornfully. "Me? That'll be the fair and frosty Friday."

Although I spent so much of my life listening to conversations which I was not meant to overhear, all at once I felt, for the first time, sickened by what I was doing. I left my listening post and tiptoed into Aunt Edna's room. I wondered if someday I would be the one who was doing the talking, while another child would be doing the listening. This gave me an unpleasantly eerie feeling. I tried on Aunt Edna's lipstick and rouge, but my heart was not in it.

When I went downstairs again, Jimmy Lorimer was just leaving. Aunt Edna went to her room and closed the door. After a while she came out and asked me if I would mind sleeping in the spare bedroom that night after all, so that was what I did.

I woke in the middle of the night. When I sat up, feeling strange because I was not in my own bed at home, I saw through the window a glancing light on the snow. I got up and peered out, and there were the northern lights whirling across the top of the sky like lightning that never descended to earth. The yard of the Brick House looked huge, a white desert, and the pale gashing streaks of light pointed up the caverns and the hollowed places where the wind had sculptured the snow.

I could not stand being alone another second, so I walked in my bare feet along the hall. From Grandfather's room came the sound of grumbling snores, and from Grandmother's room no sound at all. I stopped beside the door of Aunt Edna's room. It seemed to me that she would not mind if I entered quietly, so as not to disturb her, and crawled in beside her. Maybe she would even waken and say, "It's okay, kiddo—your dad phoned after you'd gone to sleep—they got back from Freehold all right."

Then I heard her voice, and the held-in way she was crying, and the name she spoke, as though it hurt her to speak it even in a whisper.

Like some terrified poltergeist, I flitted back to the spare room and whipped into bed. I wanted only to forget that I had heard anything, but I knew I would not forget. There arose in my mind, mysteriously, the picture of a barbaric queen, someone who had lived a long time ago. I could not reconcile this image with the known face, nor could I disconnect it. I thought of my aunt, her sturdy laughter, the way she tore into the housework, her hands and feet which she always disparagingly joked about, believing them to be clumsy. I thought of the story in the scribbler at home. I wanted to get home quickly, so I could destroy it.

Whenever Grandmother Connor was ill, she would not see any doctor except my father. She did not believe in surgery, for she thought it was tampering with the Divine Intention, and she was always afraid that Dr. Cates would operate on her without her consent. She trusted my father implicitly, and when he went into the room where she lay propped up on pillows, she would say, "Here's Ewen—now everything will be fine," which both touched and alarmed my father, who said he hoped she wasn't putting her faith in a broken reed.

Late that winter, she became ill again. She did not go into hospital, so my mother, who had been a nurse, moved down to the Brick House to look after her. My brother and I were left in the adamant care of Grandmother MacLeod. Without my mother, our house seemed like a museum, full of dead and meaningless objects, vases and gilt-framed pictures and looming furniture, all of which had to be dusted and catered to, for reasons which everyone had forgotten. I was not allowed to see Grandmother Connor, but every day after school I went to the Brick House to see my mother. I always asked impatiently, "When is Grandmother going to be better?" and my mother would reply, "I don't know, dear. Soon, I hope." But she did not sound very certain, and I imagined the leaden weeks going by like this, with her away, and Grandmother MacLeod poking her head into my bedroom doorway each morning and telling me to be sure to make my bed because a slovenly room meant a slovenly heart.

But the weeks did not go by like this. One afternoon when I arrived at the Brick House, Grandfather Connor was standing out on the front porch. I was startled, because he was not wearing his great bear coat. He wore no coat at all, only his dingy serge suit, although the day was fifteen below zero. The blown snow had sifted onto the porch and lay in thin drifts. He stood there by himself, his yellowish-white hair plumed by a wind which he seemed not to notice, his bony and still-handsome face not averted at all from the winter. He looked at me as I plodded up the path and the front steps.

"Vanessa, your grandmother's dead," he said.

Then, as I gazed at him, unable to take in the significance of what he had said, he did a horrifying thing. He gathered me into the relentless grip of his arms. He bent low over me, and sobbed against the cold skin of my face.

I wanted only to get away, to get as far away as possible and never come back. I wanted desperately to see my mother, yet I felt I could not enter the house, not ever again. Then my mother opened the front door and stood there in the doorway, her slight body shivering. Grandfather released me, straightened, became again the carved face I had seen when I approached the house.

"Father," my mother said. "Come into the house. Please."

"In a while, Beth," he replied tonelessly. "Never you mind."

My mother held out her hands to me, and I ran to her. She closed the door and led me into the living room. We both cried, and yet I think I cried mainly because she did, and because I had been shocked by my grandfather. I still could not believe that anyone I cared about could really die.

Aunt Edna came into the living room. She hesitated, looking at my mother and me. Then she turned and went back to the kitchen, stumblingly. My mother's hands made hovering movements and she half rose from the chesterfield, then she held me closely again.

"It's worse for Edna," she said. "I've got you and Roddie, and your dad."

I did not fully realise yet that Grandmother Connor would never move around this house again, preserving its uncertain peace somehow. Yet all at once I knew how it would be for Aunt Edna, without her, alone in the Brick House with Grandfather Connor. I had not known at all that a death would be like this, not only one's own pain, but the almost unbearable knowledge of that other pain which could not be reached nor lessened.

My mother and I went out to the kitchen, and the three of us sat around the oilcloth-covered table, scarcely talking but needing one another at least to be there. We heard the front door open, and Grandfather Connor came back into the house. He did not come out to the kitchen, though. He went, as though instinctively, to his old cavern. We heard him walking heavily down the basement steps.

"Edna—should we ask him if he wants to come and have some tea?" my mother said. "I hate to see him going like that—there—"

Aunt Edna's face hardened.

"I don't want to see him, Beth," she replied, forcing the words out. "I can't. Not yet. All I'd be able to think of is how he was—with her."

"Oh honey, I know," my mother said. "But you mustn't let yourself dwell on that now."

"The night Jimmy was here," my aunt said distinctly, "she asked Father to be nice, for her sake. For her sake, Beth. For the sake of all the years, if they'd meant anything at all. But he couldn't even do that. Not even that."

Then she put her head down on the table and cried in a way I had never heard any person cry before, as though there were no end to it anywhere.

I was not allowed to attend Grandmother Connor's funeral, and for this I was profoundly grateful, for I had dreaded going. The day of the funeral, I stayed alone in the Brick House, waiting for the family to return. My Uncle Terence, who lived in Toronto, was the only one who had come from a distance. Uncle Will lived in Florida, and Aunt Florence was in England, both too far away. Aunt Edna and my mother were always criticising Uncle Terence and also making excuses for him. He drank more than was good for him—this was one of the numerous fractured bones in the family skeleton which I was not supposed to know about. I was fond of him for the same reason I was fond of Grandfather's horse-trader brother, my Great-Uncle Dan—because he had gaiety and was publicly reckoned to be no good.

I sat in the dining room beside the gilt-boned cage that housed the canary. Yesterday, Aunt Edna, cleaning here, had said, "What on earth are we going to do with the canary? Maybe we can find somebody who would like it."

Grandfather Connor had immediately lit into her. "Edna, your mother liked that bird, so it's staying, do you hear?"

When my mother and Aunt Edna went upstairs to have a cigarette, Aunt Edna had said, "Well, it's dandy that he's so set on the bird now, isn't it? He might have considered that a few years earlier, if you ask me."

"Try to be patient with him," my mother had said. "He's feeling it, too."

"I guess so," Aunt Edna had said in a discouraged voice. "I haven't got Mother's patience, that's all. Not with him, nor with any man."

And I had been reminded then of the item I had seen not long before in the Winnipeg *Free Press*, on the social page, telling of the marriage of James Reilly Lorimer to Somebody-or-other. I had rushed to my mother with the paper in my hand, and she had said, "I know, Vanessa. She knows too. So let's not bring it up, eh?"

The canary, as usual, was not in a vocal mood, and I sat beside the cage dully, not caring, not even trying to prod the creature into song. I wondered if Grandmother Connor was at this very moment in heaven, that dubious place.

"She believed, Edna," my mother had said defensively. "What right have we to say it isn't so?"

"Oh, I know," Aunt Edna had replied. "But can you take it in, really, Beth?"

"No, not really. But you feel, with someone like her—it would be so awful if it didn't happen, after she'd thought like that for so long."

"She wouldn't know," Aunt Edna had pointed out.

"I guess that's what I can't accept," my mother had said slowly. "I still feel she must be somewhere."

I wanted now to hold my own funeral service for my grandmother, in the presence only of the canary. I went to the bookcase where she kept her Bible, and looked up Ecclesiastes. I intended to read the part about the mourners going about the streets, and the silver cord loosed and the golden bowl broken, and the dust returning to the earth as it was and the spirit unto God who gave it. But I got stuck on the first few lines, because it seemed to me, frighteningly, that they were being spoken in my grandmother's mild voice—*Remember now thy Creator in the days of thy youth, while the evil days come not—*

Then, with a burst of opening doors, the family had returned from the funeral. While they were taking off their coats, I slammed the Bible shut and sneaked it back into the bookcase without anyone's having noticed.

Grandfather Connor walked over to me and placed his hands on my shoulders, and I could do nothing except endure his touch.

"Vanessa—" he said gruffly, and I had at the time no idea how much it cost him to speak at all, "she was an angel. You remember that."

Then he went down to the basement by himself. No one attempted to follow him, or to ask him to come and join the rest of us. Even I, in the confusion of my lack of years, realised that this would have been an impossibility. He was, in some way, untouchable. Whatever his grief was, he did not want us to look at it and we did not want to look at it, either.

Uncle Terence went straight into the kitchen, brought out his pocket flask, and poured a hefty slug of whiskey for himself. He did the same for my mother and father and Aunt Edna.

"Oh Glory," Aunt Edna said with a sigh, "do I ever need this. All the same, I feel we shouldn't, right immediately afterwards. You know—considering how she always felt about it. Supposing Father comes up—"

"It's about time you quit thinking that way, Edna," Uncle Terence said.

Aunt Edna felt in her purse for a cigarette. Uncle Terence reached over and lit it for her. Her hands were unsteady.

"You're telling me," she said.

Uncle Terence gave me a quizzical and yet resigned look, and I knew then that my presence was placing a constraint upon them. When my father said he had to go back to the hospital, I used his departure to slip upstairs to my old post, the deserted stove-pipe hole. I could no longer eavesdrop with a clear conscience, but I justified it now by the fact that I had voluntarily removed myself from the kitchen, knowing they would not have told me to run along, not today.

"An angel," Aunt Edna said bitterly. "Did you hear what he said to Vanessa? It's a pity he never said as much to Mother once or twice, isn't it?"

"She knew how much he thought of her," my mother said.

"Did she?" Aunt Edna said. "I don't believe she ever knew he cared about her at all. I don't think I knew it myself, until I saw how her death hit him."

"That's an awful thing to say!" my mother cried. "Of course she knew, Edna."

"How would she know," Aunt Edna persisted, "if he never let on?"

"How do you know he didn't?" my mother countered. "When they were by themselves."

"I don't know, of course," Aunt Edna said. "But I have my damn shrewd suspicions."

"Did you ever know, Beth," Uncle Terence enquired, pouring himself another drink, "that she almost left him once? That was before you were born, Edna."

"No," my mother said incredulously. "Surely not."

"Yeh. Aunt Mattie told me. Apparently Father carried on for a while with some girl in Winnipeg, and Mother found out about it. She never told him she'd considered leaving him. She only told God and Aunt Mattie. The three of them thrashed it out together, I suppose. Too bad she never told him. It would've been a relief to him, no doubt, to see she wasn't all calm forgiveness."

"How could he?" my mother said in a low voice. "Oh Terence. How could he have done that? To Mother, of all people."

"You know something, Beth?" Uncle Terence said. "I think he honestly believed that about her being some kind of angel. She'd never have thought of herself like that, so I don't suppose it ever would have occurred to her that he did. But I have a notion that he felt all along she was far and away too good for him. Can you feature going to bed with an angel, honey? It doesn't bear thinking about."

"Terence, you're drunk," my mother said sharply. "As usual."

"Maybe so," he admitted. Then he burst out, "I only felt, Beth, that somebody might have said to Vanessa just now, *Look, baby, she was terrific and we thought the world of her, but let's not say angel, eh?* All this angel business gets us into really deep water, you know that?"

"I don't see how you can talk like that, Terence," my mother said, trying not to cry. "Now all of a sudden everything was her fault. I just don't see how you can."

"I'm not saying it was her fault," Uncle Terence said wearily. "That's not what I meant. Give me credit for one or two brains, Beth. I'm only saying it might have been rough for him, as well, that's all. How do any of us know what he's had to carry on his shoulders? Another person's virtues could be an awful weight to tote around. We all loved her. Whoever loved him? Who in hell could? Don't you think he knew that? Maybe he even thought sometimes it was no more than was coming to him."

"Oh—" my mother said bleakly. "That can't be so. That would be—oh, Terence, do you really think he might have thought that way?"

"I don't know any more than you do, Beth. I think he knew quite well that she had something he didn't, but I'd be willing to bet he always imagined it must be righteousness. It wasn't. It was—well, I guess it was tenderness, really. Unfair as you always are about him, Edna, I think you hit the nail on the head about one thing. I don't believe Mother ever realised he might have wanted her tenderness. Why should she? He could never show any of his own. All he could ever come out with was anger. Well, everybody to his own shield in this family. I guess I carry mine in my hip pocket. I don't know what yours is, Beth, but Edna's is more like his than you might think."

"Oh yeh?" Aunt Edna said, her voice suddenly rough. "What is it, then, if I may be so bold as to enquire?"

"Wisecracks, honey," Uncle Terence replied, very gently. "Just wisecracks."

They stopped talking, and all I could hear was my aunt's uneven breathing, with no one saying a word. Then I could hear her blowing her nose.

"Mercy, I must look like the wreck of the Hesperus," she said briskly. "I'll bet I haven't got a speck of powder left on. Never mind. I'll repair the ravages later. What about putting the kettle on, Beth? Maybe I should go down and see if he'll have a cup of tea now."

"Yes," my mother said. "That's a good idea. You do that, Edna."

I heard my aunt's footsteps on the basement stairs as she went down into Grandfather Connor's solitary place.

Many years later, when Manawaka was far away from me, in miles and in time, I saw one day in a museum the Bear Mask of the Haida Indians. It was a weird mask. The features were ugly and yet powerful. The mouth was turned down in an expression of sullen rage. The eyes were empty caverns, revealing nothing. Yet as I looked, they seemed to draw my own eyes towards them, until I imagined I could see somewhere within that darkness a look which I knew, a lurking bewilderment. I remembered then that in the days before it became a museum piece, the mask had concealed a man.

Euthanasia

To leave the world
while still game for it
planting the flower garden
expecting peas   tomatoes   corn
To leave the world
where full joy seems to lie
is nonetheless happier
than to drag drag dry
into our eighties and nineties
pretending to be real
with a false leg   an aching back
teeth intractable
eyes dim
ears only half
hearing
tongue only a stutter
memory a falter

Pray pray
for all of us
that our leap into the chasm
may be agile and willing
or at least that we know
our time of going
and persuade our children
that this has to be
just so

Why We Are Here

Some of us are here
because we were visited
at dawn
were given a third
ear

Some of us especially
are women
open
ever receiving
into

Layton says
"The womb
is such a diminutive room
in which to lie"

But some of us are here
to say *lie down*
children of men
lie down on the stiff brown stubble
at noon the ice
melting to puddles
lie down at noon
on hard soil
singing with underground
water
lie down
and let our hands bear you as rivers
to the sea's room.

Some of us are here
as messages
because in the small womb
lies all the lightning.

After Hiroshima

Not any more the visions and revelations
A voice at Emmaus, a figure of light on the hills;
Not any more the courtesan running early
To pray, and the prayer answered in act: an astonished tomb.

We see no mysteries; miracles are not accepted,
The beating rain bears no messages for man;
Though sun may still burn hot, searing the skin
No hearts dare listen while fear stirs the womb.

What the right hand doeth, stirring the pot of evil—
The hydrogen brew; the left knows not, is sleeping;
If the mind asserts, the heart dare not conjecture;
The picture upon the wall is unveiled, but dare not speak.

Not any more the visions and revelations:
Only in brief flashes is light received, good news.
Only a child's belief, rocked in a cradle of doubt,
Can prophesy our safety; illuminate our hope.

Improvisation on an Old Theme

If I must go, let it be easy, slow
The curve complete, and a sure swerve
To the goal. Let it be slow and sweet
To know how leaf consumes its time,
How petal sucks to the sun's heat
Or as old bones, settling into soil,
Eyes too remote for earth's light
Set on a solar circle whose bright
Business brims the universe.

Let me know well how the winds blow
Smoky in autumn with leaf reek;
And summer's sleek surrender,
Torching the maple; let my branches sigh
For snow, and in a muffled mantle, let me go.

Keep me for quiet. Save me ever from
Disastrous ending sounding without drum,
No decent exhalation of the breath—
The dazzling violence of atomic death.

The Uninvited

Always a third one's there
where any two are walking out
along a river-bank   so mirror-still
sheathed in sheets
of sky   pillows of cloud—
their footprints crunch the hardening earth
their eyes delight in trees   stripped clean
winter-prepared
with only the rose-hips red
and the plump fingers of sumach

And always between the two
(scuffing the leaves, laughing
and fingers locked)
goes a third lover   his or hers
who walked this way with one or other   once
flung back the head   snapped branches of dark pine
in armfuls   before snowfall

I walk beside you
trace
a shadow's shade
skating on silver
hear
another voice
singing under ice

Threshold

This is the door: the archway where I stopped
To gaze a moment over well-loved fields
Before I sought the fire within, the bright
Gold sunlight on the floor, and over all,
Upstairs and down, some clear voice singing out
Music I knew long since, but had forgot.
This is the door, the threshold of my way
Where I must watch the early afternoon
Cast shadows on the road of morning's light,
The gardens and the fields of noonday sun.
This is the door, where others quickly pass,
But where my feet seek out a resting-place—
Balanced for this brief time between the thought
Of what the heart has known, and must yet know.

Other

1

Men prefer an island
With its beginning ended:
Undertone of waves
Trees overbended.

Men prefer a road
Circling, shell-like
Convex and fossiled
Forever winding inward.

Men prefer a woman
Limpid in sunlight
Held as a shell
On a sheltering island...

Men prefer an island.

2

But I am mainland
O I range
From upper country to the inner core:
From sageland, brushland, marshland
To the sea's floor.

Show me an orchard where I have not slept,
A hollow where I have not wrapped
The sage about me, and above, the still
Stars clustering
Over the ponderosa pine, the cactus hill.

Tell me a time
I have not loved,
A mountain left unclimbed:
A prairie field
Where I have not furrowed my tongue,
Nourished it out of the mind's dark places;
Planted with tears unwept
And harvested as friends, as faces.

O find me a dead-end road
I have not trodden
A logging road that leads the heart away
Into the secret evergreen of cedar roots
Beyond sun's farthest ray—
Then, in a clearing's sudden dazzle,
There is no road; no end; no puzzle.

But do not show me! For I know
The country I caress:
A place where none shall trespass
None possess:
A mainland mastered
From its inaccess.

* * * *

Men prefer an island.

JACK LUDWIG

Requiem for Bibul

Once upon a time—if we counted time not by calendars but by assimilated history and scientific change, I'd be tempted to say four or five thousand years ago—before total war and all-out war, before death camps, Nagasaki, before fusion and fission, jets, moon shots, astronauts, luniks in orbit, before antibiotics, polio vaccine, open-heart surgery, before TV, garburetors, and other wonders of automation, before dead-faced hoods on motorcycles, dead-faced beatniks on maldecycles; once upon *that* kind of time lived a boy and his horse. The year was 1939. The boy and the horse are both dead.

This is no pastoral tale.

Twenty years late, counting time by the calendar, I write you of this boy Bibul and his horse Malkeh, of Bibul's ambition and his sad, sad end. In time-sorrowed perspective I record for you the imprint Bibul left on my mind and feeling: his ticlike blink, his coal-black hair in bangs over his forehead, his emery-cloth shaver's shadow, his ink-stained mouth, his immutable clothes that wouldn't conform to style or the seasons—always black denim relief-style pants whitened by wear and washing, always a brown pebbled cardigan coiled at the wrists and elbows with unraveled wool, always a leather cap with bent visor, split seams, matching the color and texture of Bibul's hair. And old ruined Malkeh, scorned before lamented, making her daily round under Bibul's urging, dragging his creak of a fruit peddler's wagon through Winnipeg's "island" slum north of the Canadian Pacific Railway yards.

Bibul peddled while my time burned: in 1939 all of us high school boys were owlish with sixteen- and seventeen-year-old speculation and almost missed seeing this Bibul, all foxy with world-weary finagling. We were out to save the world; Bibul, a buck. Hip deep in reality, trying to beat tricky suppliers, weaselly competitors, haggling customers, Bibul couldn't believe in us vaguesters. Peddling had forced him to see, hear and judge everything. By his practical measure, we were simply unreal. We'd speculate; Bibul would respond with "*Yeh-yeh,*" the Yiddish double affirmative that makes a negative. He didn't have to say a word, or raise that skeptical eyebrow, or even frown with that tic. His smell alone argued a reality out of reach of our politely neutral, Lux, Lifebuoy, Vitalis middle-class sweetness: "effluvium Bibul" we called that mixture of squashed berries, bad turnips, dank pine apple-crates, straw, chickens, sad old horsy Malkeh. Bibul had a grand gesture to sweep away our irrelevance, a sudden movement of the hand like a farmwife's throwing feed to chickens, his nose sniffing disgust, his sour mouth giving out a squelching sound, "*Aaaa.*" Sometimes he sounded like a goat, other times a baby lamb; just "*Aaaa,*" but enough to murder our pushy pretensions.

We were a roomful of competitive sharks—math sharks, physics sharks, English, Latin, history sharks—secretly, often openly sure that we surpassed our teachers in brains and know-how. Joyfully arrogant, we shook off the restricting label of "high school student," considering ourselves pros—mathematicians, scientists, writers, artists. In our own minds we had already graduated from the university, had passed through Toronto or Oxford, were entangled in public controversies with the great names in our respective fields, ending right but humble, modestly triumphant. But where was Bibul in this league? As loudly as we pros hollered, Bibul heard nothing. He only yawned, slouched, even snoozed, gave out with that killing "*Yeh-yeh,*" poked his grayish nose into his peddler's notebook red with reality's ooze of tomato.

"Bibul," we'd try to break in on him, "aren't you interested in semantics? Don't you care for the coming intellectual revolution?

Once and for all, are you for Count Korzybski or are you against him?"

"*Aaaa*," was Bibul's response, and that chicken-feeding gesture waved us back to our ivory towers. Bibul turned to reality with a lick of his indelible-pencil's tip and a purple inscription in his book of life.

"You nuddin' bud gids," he'd say impatiently if we insisted on disturbing his audit. "A 'ell of a lod you guys know aboud live."

We'd jeer and mock, which made no impression on Bibul, nor did much for us. Weren't we the kings of St. John's High School? Even if Bibul wasn't very active, he was still one of us on the top floor, dominating with us the giants and dwarfs living the underground life amid blazing forges and screeching lathes in the school basement, second-generation Canadians joyously illiterate, English having to fend for itself in their houses, a poor second to Ukrainian or Polish or German; or the salt-of-the-earth commercial students, blond and blue-eyed, clearly dedicated to the sensible life, who heard our loud violent arguments and shuddered in silence and good taste.

We might have been kings, but how could anybody crown Bibul? We ran the yearbook, but it, sad for Bibul's talents, was printed neither in Yiddish nor Hebrew, and on Bibul's "island" who had mastered English? We wanted him to debate, but peddling had made him overexcited; wrought up, he stammered, angry, he slobbered—hindrances to the winning of arguments. Tone-deaf, he was no candidate for the glee club; a business man through and through, he had no time for politics. At sports he was terrible; he couldn't swim a stroke, or skate, was flubby-knuckled at baseball, slashingly pigeon-toed at soccer, kamikaze going over a hurdle. He had no time for women in his life. Malkeh and the ladies who bought from him were the only females Bibul knew; these customers whom he called with a little, if not much, affection *schnorrers*, pigs.

In recognition of his great talent, we made him room treasurer.

After school, while we theoreticians sprawled on boulevards and took pleasure from the long-limbed, large-breasted twelfth-grade girls giving the lie to an educator's pious wish that the serge tunic neutralize the female form, Bibul hurried off to Malkeh, that wagon open-pored and gaping for paint, the running of a gauntlet of schnorrers avid for a beet or turnip to fill an empty pot. And early on a morning, when we theoreticians-turned-lovers, wearied after a long night of girls, sat in the Street Railway waiting house knocking ourselves out over my noisy reading of Panurge's adventure with the Lady of Paris, Bibul, up and dressed at 4 A.M., waited with Malkeh for the fruit row to open and the struggle for possession of the bruised fruit and battered vegetables he'd have to wrest from ancient wizened trickster peddlers and their muscular sons so that his schnorrers would have something concrete to haggle over later in the day.

Lost in abstraction, and me, I thought little of Bibul in those days. He was a clown. A mark. A butt. The peddling was part of the sad, desperate struggle for money every family in the Depression knew. Bibul was the oldest of four children, his widowed ma supporting them on what she could make out of a tiny grocery store, doing the best she could, the dear lady, and known throughout the island as the "Golden Thumb" and the "Adder," the latter reference ambiguous, meaning either snakes or computation, Bibul's ma being famous for a mathematical theorem that said 5 + 6 = 12, or 13, whichever was higher.

Not till the year of our graduation did I discover why Bibul peddled with such dedication, why he rode out like a teen-age Don Quixote to do battle with those abusive, haggling, thieving schnorrers.

What a riding out that was! His paintless wagon listed like a sinking ship, moved with the sound of fiddles scraped rosinless in a concert by deaf mutes, its wheels' circles successfully squared, a few spokes missing from each, its seat a tatter of leatherette bulged at the ends like a horsehair cream puff, its wilted greens and culled fruit lorded over by Bibul's faultless-in-his-favor scales, rusted fistlike weights, a battered tin scoop more dented than a defeated

World War I veteran's helmet. For such a wagon, what was more fitting than a progress through the island under the leadership of a nag like Malkeh!

As beat up as Don Quixote's Rosinante would look next to elegant Pegasus, that's how Malkeh would look next to Rosinante: she was U-shaped in side view, as if she'd been ridden by the fattest knight in heaviest armor; she sagged like a collapsed sofa with its stuffing hanging low. She was bare as buffed mohair, her shoulders tanned from the rub of reins, her color an unbelievable combination of rust, maroon, purple, brown, found elsewhere only in ancient sun-drenched velvets. Her tail was a worn discarded feather boa picked almost clean. Like a badly carpentered table, all four of her legs were of assorted lengths, which made her move by shuffling, like a pair of aged soft-shoe dancers making a final farewell. Her hoofs were fringed with fuzzy hairs like a frayed fiddle bow abandoned to rain and sun, her horseshoes were thin as dimes, rusty as the metal hinges on her wagon's tail gate.

Her faded yellow horse collar and harness once sat on a czarist artillery horse, but now, padless, dry, broken, reknotted, supported Malkeh in poor style, fitting much like the suits handed up by Bibul's competitors' muscular sons to their tiny fathers. To encourage her to see out of her old eyes, Bibul flatteringly covered them at the sides with a pair of snappy black racing-horse blinkers trimmed with shiny silver rivets, a touch to Malkeh's décor like a monocle in the eye of a Bowery bum.

Out of loyalty to this Malkeh, Bibul let his wagon go to ruin: a wagon could be covered over with paint or varnish, but poor mortal Malkeh, where was the therapy or camouflage to hide from the world what *she* really was?

She was the horse version of *The Dying Gaul.* While Malkeh lived on her island she wasn't subject to the reality of horse hierarchy, but on a main thoroughfare like Salter Street her submarginal subproletariat position was exposed. High-stepping T. Eaton Company horses, glossy-flanked, curried, combed, middle-class cousins of aristocratic thoroughbreds seen only on race tracks and in stables, spurned Malkeh as they sped past, their harnesses shiny with saddle soap, their hoofs steel-ringing, their heads up, their traces white as snow, their tails prinked out with red ribbons, their wagons elegant as chariots, freshly painted, glowing blue-black, red, white, and gold where it counted, their drivers uniform and uniformed, not like sloppy Bibul. Horses like these had blankets, slept in fancy T. Eaton stables, ate oats from an unfaded green feed bag, not the ripped postman's pouch Bibul filled with bad lettuce, carrot tops, shriveled beets wisped over with a sign of hay. Their snubbing was a denial that Malkeh was a horse. Even the heavy, powerful working-class Percherons, inexorably destined for life to the smell of the garbage scows they pulled through the city, refused to acknowledge kinship with Malkeh, speeding up without any urging, turning into a can-ridden back lane with relief, much as a person at a high-toned party successfully hides from a waiter who turns out to be a close relative.

I saw her only once, when Bibul brought her to school. A crowd gathered, some to gawk, some to cluck, some to find cause for letters to the editor. The principal happened to look out. Malkeh died a long time ago, but her memory is gnomically preserved in a memorial tablet that went up early next day and says clearly "No Parking at Any Time."

That was the first and last time Bibul brought Malkeh to school.

Not that the island was without hazards. Perhaps Bibul had put blinders on Malkeh to keep the old animal from seeing reality too clearly with whatever sight she still had left in her eyes. Those schnorrers, bare feet stuck hurriedly into their husbands' felt house slippers, wearing nightgowns at four in the afternoon, their hair uncombed, their hands deep in housecoat and apron pockets in a gesture like stick-up men's, pennies and silver tightly clenched, prizes Bibul could get with bargains, fast talk, tempting, threats, guile. Singly they watched for him, in concert they plotted unbeatable stratagems, their motto simple: Pay little, get much.

To the victor went the spoiled spoils.

"Giddy ahb, Malgeh," Bibul would holler from his high seat, and the schnorrers knew that war was on.

Into the lists Malkeh dragged the keening wagon, onto the island in ruins like a medieval town (Canadian history is short, but our buildings add spice by getting older faster). Foundationless houses sagged, leaned at angles to astound Pisa, some north, some south, giving an effect of pure craziness, what kids might have built with assorted-sized decks of cards. Gates tipsy as Malkeh's wagon swung on one hinge from a last lost post; dry, cracking wood fences leaned in surrender toward the ground, begging like old men in sight of a grave to be allowed to fall the rest of the way; windows were tar-paper patched, like pirates' eyes, and ominous as the blackness left in the streets by uninsured fires.

Behind every window or screen opaque with dust, behind every door splintered from kids' kicking waited the schnorrers, trying to make Bibul anxious, make him sweat a little, a cinch for persistent hagglers.

"Ebbles, ebbles, den boundz f'a quadder!" Bibul shouted.

The schnorrers didn't move.

Unflustered, unfooled, Bibul used his phony war time well, popping into his mouth the only three unspotted cherries in his entire stock. Malkeh, for her bit, sighing and groaning, panting but pulling, dragged the exposed tin rims of the wheels off the street and into the frost heaves and crevices of the muddy back lane which Bibul and his customers had silently agreed was the Compleat Battlefield, Bibul because the cloudlike stench of chicken droppings and horse dung hanging over the lane was unbeatable camouflage for whatever imperfection time and decay might bring his produce, his schnorrers because the cramped quarters of a narrow lane made scale tampering easier for their anxious old hands, detection difficult, filching not so.

"Whoa beg, whoa der, Malgeh," Bibul ordered, and there among ripped mattresses resembling enormous wads of steel wool, in a bone yard of Model T Fords, Malkeh finally halted.

Dogs came yapping from all directions, cats hissed from rust-streaked iron roof tops, frightened pigeons whirred into the air, wheeling high over sunbeaten stables, returning to their places like grandstand fans anxious to be close to the scene of scuffle.

Bibul's ticlike blink was a cover for all expression. He looked blanker than the Sphinx. He faked a brow-furrowing entry into his book, peeled an orange, scratched himself variously and thoroughly. The schnorrers couldn't stand the suspense. Dead was their united front. A few broke ranks and, already cursing Bibul's bad prices, shuffled out in a gait to match Malkeh's.

Horseflies, the pickings so sparse they had to drop their high standards and declare Malkeh a possible host, left the poor banquet of the uncovered garbage cans—each lid long commandeered to serve as target in the minor-league jousts of the schnorrers' knightly kids—and, under cover of the schnorrers sneakily advancing to do Bibul battle, launched assault on Malkeh's weak flank. In a second, both boy and horse were under siege.

The attack came swiftly: stealthily, deftly, a red-haired old woman flipped two-cent oranges into the one-cent bins, her rasp of a voice trying to get Bibul to look up at the sky and predict weather; her accomplice meanwhile made a great display of finding a terrific buy.

"Boyaboyaboy, f'a change you god good tings in this stinkin' wagon," she said shamelessly.

Bibul's ticlike blink was a camera shutter ready for mischief, and snapped the entire action.

"Give over here dat bag," he said gruffly. "Mizzuz, *yoisher*, show a liddle resdraind," he scolded the old innocents watching the oranges fall back into the proper bin.

A pair of raspberry hands crunched lettuce greens. "How much you give off f' damaged goods?" the criminal hollered, while still wiping lettuce juice off on her apron.

The red-haired old woman was set on getting oranges. "Robber, black-hearted robber," she cried out, shaking a fist under Bibul's disapproving nose. "Perls d' fruit man, a father who supports eight growin' kids and a sister in Russia, Perls charges two coppers cheaper for fresher and firmer, so ha come, ha? Ha come?"

"My oniges are Sundgizd, Blue Gooze," came back Bibul, a sucker for brand names. "Berls's oniges grow on ebble drees."

With a slamming of doors and a shuffle of feet the schnorrers came now in full force, wave after wave, surrounding Bibul's wagon, pressing fruit, squeezing, poking, tapping, filling the air with shrieks and curses that urged the pigeonhearted pigeons high to the sky. Like a bucket brigade, the ladies passed fruit the length of the wagon, each nose a compulsory inspection station. Some—baseball fans, no doubt—tried the hidden-ball trick with Bibul's apples; others, proud of what teeth they had left, showed off a little by nipping fruit as it passed by.

For each bite Bibul took his due.

"Schnorrers dad youz are," he yelled, imposing and collecting his fine, "you god no gare vor my brovids? You eadin' ub all my brovids!"

"Don' be s'independent," said the red-haired one, fruitlessly after a fistful of cherries, "don' hold yourself big. You' fadder ain' no doctor, he ain' no mayor!"

Bibul was a lone guard defending his fortress from desperate pillagers; ubiquitous as Churchill, many-handed as Shiva, he had to be compassionate as Schweitzer. Though I didn't know what Bibul's dedication to peddling was all about, the schnorrers did: Bibul was saving up to become a rabbi. Bibul immersed himself in the practical, pedestrian, material life because of a Great Cause—the Yeshiva in New York, eventual immersion in a spiritual life dedicated to suffering mankind.

How the schnorrers used that Great Cause in their war with Bibul! It was all double: in sincerity they poured out their hearts to him; an educated boy, soon to be a rabbi, maybe he'd understand *their* side—the husband who had taken off and never come back, the bad-hearted rich relatives, the ungrateful kids, the treacherous friends, root, trunk, branch of a Jewish Seven Deadly Sins. They dizzied him with complicated stories, unsettled his strong stomach with demonstrations of human frailty—missing teeth, crossed eyes, wens, tumors, needed operations.

As a bonus to sincerity they hoped the tales would divert Bibul long enough for their aprons to fill with filched fruit.

Crying real tears, Bibul would free an apricot from a fist already stained with cherry.

"A religious you call yourself?" the caught thief howled. "God should strike me dead if I stole ever in my life one thing!"

Glancing up at the sky, she moved closer to the other ladies: who knew what kind of pull with God a boy to be a rabbi had?

"Bibul, *boychik*," cooed this Mrs. Fenson, bleached a little but not yet forty, without a man since her husband disappeared into the harvest lands of Saskatchewan years before. "Give off ten cents on this here dozen, eh, doll? I can show plenty good appreciation."

Bibul shuddered a No. There were some things in this material world even the Great Cause did not justify.

For their part, his schnorrers prayed God to give Bibul good enough ears to hear out their incriminating bill of particulars against the human race, bad eyes to miss seeing what their energetic hands were doing; and they cursed fate when Bibul's unaffected eyes snapped them filching. After a day of listening to lamentation, was there anything Bibul could hear that would amaze him?

"My brudder's second wibe's kid wid da hump in back god already her tird miscarriage, Bibul," he'd hear, and a second later, "Ha c'n ya cha'ge two cends a pond f'a busted wadermelon?"—this to the accompanying sound of a melon being smartly cracked against the side of the wagon.

"Bay ub, bay ub." Bibul would rise to his full height on the wagon's seat, like a soapbox orator trying to sway these masses.

That's when the curses changed from rain to hail, the moment for desperation measures—pinching, throwing a kiss, snatching a potato, gulping a cherry, pit and all. But Bibul was through. A loving kick woke Malkeh, a swish of the broken whip banished her horseflies. The swaying tin scoop clattered retreat, the creaking wagon mocked the defeated schnorrers cursing boy and horse down through all possible generations.

Was it any wonder, then, that when we sharks, all hot for culture, oozing ideology, long on judgments, short on facts, turned our abstract faces toward Bibul, he responded with that "*Aaaa*"? What was there in our books and ideas to compete with a schnorrer's lament? Now I know what that "*Aaaa*" meant in part: "*Aaaa*" translated "When I was a child I spake as a child" (may Bibul forgive me for invoking St. Paul!) or "You nuddin' bud gids." "*Aaaa*" said "vanity of vanities; all is vanity" and, in explanation of Bibul's giving himself to Mammon for a term so that he might give the rest to Abraham, Isaac, and Jacob, "To everything there is a season, and a time to every purpose under the heaven."

The sharks vaguely yearned for the Higher Life; Bibul alone had a concrete goal, a building in a specific city, New York. Every knightly thrust and parry with an unqueenly schnorrer, every cull of orange he sold, every bruised apple brought him that much closer to the Yeshiva.

On graduation day at St. John's, Bibul was already half a rabbi. Gone were the familiar cardigan and accompanying accessories. Bibul wore a brand-new serge suit. His sideburns were religious enough to be called side curls, the emery-cloth shadow was lengthened. His eyes shone with a fervor no schnorrer had ever seen. He looked beautiful, incredibly happy.

"Damorrow," he said in a low secretive voice, "I go d' Yeshiva in New Yorg. I wanna say goo'by, Joe."

"New York?" I said. "A city that big? Aren't you a little afraid?"

"*Aaaa*." Bibul gave me that wave of his. "Wadz t' be sgared?"

"You're a stranger. Winnipeg's a village compared with New York."

"*Aaaa*. Zame ding. Beoble iz beoble."

"What about Malkeh?"

"Berls da beddler robbed me. I gave Malgeh away t' him. Da groog knew I was goin' d' New Yorg."

"Bibul," I said enthusiastically, "good luck to you. Be a good rabbi!"

"*Aaaa*," he said with the usual flourish, his last word to me then or ever.

That fall we sharks entered the university, and Canada the war. Winnipeg was transformed, full of air crew trainees from places known to me before only through postage stamps; yellow skins, black, red, brown, Maori tribesmen from New Zealand, Bushmen from Australia, strange-sounding South Africans, sculpture-faced Indians thronged the city's streets and beer parlors. But far off in New York, Bibul, who'd known war with his schnorrers since his thirteenth year, paid no attention to this latest struggle, his mind committed to the study of Torah and Talmud, his spare time involved in a fruit-selling job among the East Side schnorrers around New York's Essex Street market. His old customers, a little cash to speculate with now that the Depression seemed ended, haggled halfheartedly with old man Perls and old Malkeh, the one mercifully deaf, the other almost totally blind.

Once in a long while I checked in at Bibul's mother's store and, gleaning news of Bibul, let her weigh me up a light pound of corned beef. She wore her hair Buster Brown, carried a huge buxom body on little feet tucked into gray-white tennis shoes.

She shoved a letter at me.

"Look how a educated boy writes," she said, pugnaciously proud. "Who but a rabbi could understand such hard words?"

She pulled it back before I could give an opinion.

"See him only, look, look." She pushed a picture at my eyes.

Bibul huddled against a bare Williamsburg wall, grinning the same grin as three other Bibuls in the picture, all of them bearded and wild as Russians, in black beaver hats bought with money they had earned tutoring the Americanized grandchildren of rich Hasidim.

"Some boy, my Bibul," his mother called to me as I was leaving.

Winter passed; the war grew grimmer. Spring was beautiful; the war more dreadful. Summer was very hot in New York, where Bibul divided his time between the Yeshiva and Essex Street's schnorrers. For days, the temperature was in the high humid nineties. Bibul had never known such heat. He couldn't study, sleep, sell. In desperation he took himself one evening to the Y, forgetting, in the heat, that he had never learned to swim.

An attendant, going off duty, warned Bibul away, told him not to enter the pool. Who can be blind to Bibul's response?

"*Aaaa*," and that gesture.

He drowned.

His schnorrers, being told, wept and lamented. We sharks, even in the midst of the war's casualties, were moved and stricken.

Bibul was the first of us to die.

I cannot find Bibul's like in Winnipeg today.

Somebody waved a T-square wand over the old island, and the ninety-degree angle, unknown a few thousand years ago, in Bibul's time, has made its appearance there. Progress pretends Bibul's island never existed: the back lanes are paved, paint has been sloshed all over the bare wood fences. When the green gave out, the painters, unflustered, turned to brown. Bibul's world has left signs of itself: a clothesline pole, exhausted from long years of supporting soggy fleece-lined underwear, seems ready to give up the ghost; an outside staircase, impermanent as a hangman's scaffold, still mocks the fire commissioner who asked for safety and got greater danger.

Malkeh is dead. The wagon fell to pieces. Motorized peddlers in trucks like Brink's cars zoom through the island late at night with the remnants of produce picked over by ringed and braceleted upper-middle-class hands on the day route: River Heights, Silver Heights, Garden City; places of Togetherness, Betterness, Spotlessness, the answers Comfort has given the questions of Civilization.

"Apples, apples, two pounds for a quarter," cry the peddlers, but not too loudly, and the women once poor enough to be schnorrers—few are left—and the women living in the rebuilt T-squared houses look over the produce, ironically like Bibul's old rejects because of prior pawing, buy a little, haggle not at all, or withdraw with a snub at peddlers, a bow in favor of the superior refrigeration of the supermarkets.

Throughout Bibul's city, cars pass in unending gaggle, the drivers great speedsters with no goal for their horsepower. The mayor tells the people to "Think Big" and hang many flags and buntings. Slums like Bibul's island and the city hall are doomed; Winnipeg is obviously a better place in which to live; who doesn't salute the coming of prosperity?

But the fact remains, I cannot find Bibul's like in Winnipeg today. And that is why, here and now, in this, his and my city, I write you this requiem for Bibul, for his face, for his Cause, his tic, his wave, his "*Aaaa.*" In love and the joy of remembering, I sing you this Bibul and all that's past and passing but not to come.

When the city hall is torn down they will build Winnipeg a new one, but where, oh, where shall we find more Bibuls?

BRIAN MacKINNON

I Told the Circle of Holy Women

On the
top floor
below the electric cross
where we would
later stand together
above the city
near the junction of two rivers
He and I
on New Year's
Day
dressed for church and
Sunday school
with itchy gray flannels
for Saint Andrew's
I let go
of his hand-for-the-moment
and followed;
my little sister, my mother
and I, we followed
my father, the surgeon,
the bone surgeon, the one
who opened up the sick people
and took care of the poor,
the chief of surgery
with raven-black hair
and moustached face;
as we entered the
black and white circle of women
we bore his arms like wings
I caught the rise and
fall of his unbroken voice
as he spoke clearly

to the cloaked women
whose voices carried the
accents of French Canada,
they were in awe of his healing powers,
it was obvious to them
that his powers were Christ given,
I said "Happy New Year, Sister!"
to each as was the custom this day
among the tall shadows of robed women
who hung long silver crosses from their necks
I, being the eldest and the first born son,
was asked if
I was going to follow in my father's
footsteps?
I told the circle of holy women
again and again that I would.

The Bedside Stories

The bedside stories
    have been rewritten into bedside horrors

The telling father once told
    bedtime stories to the listening son

But there are no known or unknown tall tales
    that this childman can begin
    to tell the fatherchild ravaged

At this bedside, bedtide.

KENNETH McROBBIE

Making It Light

That glare on the clouds is a city
                                        of five or more hundred
thousand people striking matches,
                                        soft ashes of dark between.
—Warm my hands, luminous little heart-beats!
Say I am here, one after the other.

In the space of daylight, round
                                        and smokeless
you strike the light or are blown sideways,
                                        blue tear of flame
emptying into an air tremor
a black finger stealing down your wood

—or huge against the night, descending
                                        all in white:
unchanging seed, hot and hollow heart,
                                        diminishing the dark
which brushes scattered feathers of fire
over my eyes long after.

Dust Before Rain

Neutral earth is coming
at me from every side
        of shadow,
grainy clouds stirred up by the wind
turning to blood red
the tall radio beacons;
it sifts through the windowframes
        of the last houses
on the prairie's rim.

Earth is in my breathing
each nostril outlining,
        grinding under
my hand at its writing,
settling over my reading,
        into my scalp,
on dust-dry polished palms;
it underlines my chin.
The dark has come visiting.

Never dying; not free to live.
Like air, a kind of nothing
        yet tangible,
working down to the skin
rubbed into the pale heel's ball,
        its shiny netting
in the foot's arch filling in
particulars, with a reverting
so general something.

So easily stirred, when
large raindrops with
        their puff
and noise of taps' turning-on
from nowhere come
        thudding down; its
sudden dark grass starts
up from their rising splash;

rain, departing as easily
leaving the dust of earth
      stretched out
like a drum to the horizon,
finely lined and seeping
      through pores, its
skin growing, breathing.

ANGELA MEDWID

O Pen Let Her

Nearly everything these days is so stifled. I think **There's something in the air**

pruning our feelings like we're so many

potted plants and we both know

such fragile things.

HELP I say to my voices.

We're listening. They say. But I wonder.

They're off doing their own thing, like news reporting:

Man still missing after mill explosion

Man gets three years for sexual assaults

Same man suspected in

three bank heists

A Bad man

So I go to a movie; hope for some relief. There's a woman

at a sink, her **brain filled with babies**

There's another woman, obsessed, her entire life is a

Quest for an elusive beauty

amongst the rubble. Good luck I say . . .

The next scene; the one we've all been waiting for. The one we've heard so much about. A love scene? Guess again. No. It's something less embarrassing....

It's **A boring** **BIG** **MEAN**

Death Everything **turns red**

and remember..... **films never lie**

Walk home. Hey voices, is it time

FOR A LOVE AFFAIR?

Your choice. Walk through the days covered in

'Zombie powder' or follow

A trail of tragedy as you

race to hide behind THE GREAT WALL OF SILENCE

Beyond which

'IT'S ALL LIES'

But this offer is very clear.

YOU WON'T BELIEVE how easy Making contact is.

It's awkward at first I know. You may FEEL LIKE A DUMMY

You may say with these hands? Just don't give up.

Keep repeating to yourself It can't happen, but it doesn't keep me from trying. I'm the eternal optimist."[1]

[1]Pearl McGonigal, Lieutenant Governor of Manitoba.

AUDREY POETKER

touching home

sprinting along side of you
holding back against
the wind   letting you run
strong   head high
into the sweet summer
the grass is too high
field mice run & grasshoppers
pop like corn
down our path

& if you won
it was no sacrifice
but sacrament
in the days when you touching home
& me touching you
meant safe

susie is here
to complete our trinity
of youth   standing
on each others' shoulders
so high we see eternity
from the tire tied
to the old maple
by the lilac bushes

i remember brownie barking
the world tilting
at our laughter
at onkel john's laugh booming
out from the kitchen

now in your garden
of celestial calm
how infantile i must seem
to you   sister
writhing & genuflecting
at each lash of wind
but it's not so much
the words as that each
one finds a grief
to centre on
let's loose a string
of vowels around our necks
& speak of whales & seals
& how we liked to swing
when we were young
& in the raised crosses
& stone tablets
chisel the haiku

of our names

SINCLAIR ROSS

Cornet at Night

The wheat was ripe and it was Sunday. "Can't help it—I've got to cut," my father said at breakfast. "No use talking. There's a wind again and it's shelling fast."

"Not on the Lord's Day," my mother protested. "The horses stay in the stables where they belong. There's church this afternoon and I intend to ask Louise and her husband home for supper."

Ordinarily my father was a pleasant, accommodating little man, but this morning his wheat and the wind had lent him sudden steel. "No, today we cut," he met her evenly. "You and Tom go to church if you want to. Don't bother me."

"If you take the horses out today I'm through—I'll never speak to you again. And this time I mean it."

He nodded. "Good—if I'd known I'd have started cutting wheat on Sundays years ago."

"And that's no way to talk in front of your son. In the years to come he'll remember."

There was silence for a moment and then, as if in its clash with hers his will had suddenly found itself, my father turned to me.

"Tom, I need a man to stook for a few days and I want you to go to town tomorrow and get me one. The way the wheat's coming along so fast and the oats nearly ready too I can't afford the time. Take old Rock. You'll be safe with him."

But ahead of me my mother cried, "That's one thing I'll not stand for. You can cut your wheat or do anything else you like yourself, but you're not interfering with him. He's going to school tomorrow as usual."

My father bunched himself and glared at her. "No, for a change he's going to do what I say. The crop's more important than a day at school."

"But Monday's his music lesson day—and when will we have another teacher like Miss Wiggins who can teach him music too?"

"A dollar for lessons and the wheat shelling! When I was his age I didn't even get to school."

"Exactly," my mother scored, "and look at you today. Is it any wonder I want him to be different?"

He slammed out at that to harness his horses and cut his wheat, and away sailed my mother with me in her wake to spend an austere half-hour in the dark, hot, plushy little parlour. It was a kind of vicarious atonement, I suppose, for we both took straight-backed leather chairs, and for all of the half-hour stared across the room at a big pansy-bordered motto on the opposite wall: *As for Me and My House We Will Serve the Lord.*

At last she rose and said, "Better run along and do your chores now, but hurry back. You've got to take your bath and change your clothes, and maybe help a little getting dinner for your father."

There was a wind this sunny August morning, tanged with freedom and departure, and from his stall my pony Clipper whinnied for a race with it. Sunday or not, I would ordinarily have had my gallop anyway, but today a sudden welling-up of social and religious conscience made me ask myself whether one in the family like my father wasn't bad enough. Returning to the house, I merely said that on such a fine day it seemed a pity to stay inside. My mother heard but didn't answer. Perhaps her conscience too was working. Perhaps after being worsted in the skirmish with my father, she was in no mood for granting dispensations. In any case I had to take my bath as usual, put on a clean white shirt, and change my overalls for knicker corduroys.

They squeaked, those corduroys. For three months now they had been spoiling all my Sundays. A sad, muted, swishing little squeak, but distinctly audible. Every step and there it was, as if I needed to be oiled. I had to wear them to church and Sunday-school; and after service, of course, while the grown-ups stood about gossiping, the other boys discovered my affliction. I sulked and fumed, but there was nothing to be done. Corduroys that had cost four-fifty simply couldn't be thrown away till they were well worn-out. My mother warned me that if I started sliding down the stable roof, she'd patch the seat and make me keep on wearing them.

With my customary little bow-legged sidle I slipped into the kitchen again to ask what there was to do. "Nothing but try to behave like a Christian and a gentleman," my mother answered stiffly. "Put on a tie, and shoes and stockings. Today your father is just about as much as I can bear."

"And then what?" I asked hopefully. I was thinking that I might take a drink to my father, but dared not as yet suggest it.

"Then you can stay quiet and read—and afterwards practise your music lesson. If your Aunt Louise should come she'll find that at least I bring my son up decently."

It was a long day. My mother prepared the midday meal as usual, but, to impress upon my father the enormity of his conduct, withdrew as soon as the food was served. When he was gone, she and I emerged to take our places at the table in an atmosphere of unappetizing righteousness. We didn't eat much. The food was cold, and my mother had no heart to warm it up. For relief at last she said, "Run along and feed the chickens while I change my dress. Since we aren't going to service today we'll read Scripture for a while instead."

And Scripture we did read, Isaiah, verse about, my mother in her black silk dress and rhinestone brooch, I in my corduroys and Sunday shoes that pinched. It was a very august afternoon, exactly like the tone that had persisted in my mother's voice since breakfast time. I think I might have openly rebelled, only for the hope that by compliance I yet might win permission for the trip to town with Rock. I was inordinately proud that my father had suggested it, and for his faith in me forgave him even Isaiah and the plushy afternoon. Whereas with my mother, I decided, it was a case of downright bigotry.

We went on reading Isaiah, and then for a while I played hymns on the piano. A great many hymns—even the ones with awkward sharps and accidentals that I'd never tried before—for, fearing visitors, my mother was resolved to let them see that she and I were uncontaminated by my father's sacrilege. But among these likely visitors was my Aunt Louise, a portly, condescending lady married to a well-off farmer with a handsome motor-car, and always when she came it was my mother's vanity to have me play for her a waltz or reverie, or *Holy Night* sometimes with variations. A man-child and prodigy might eclipse the motor-car. Presently she roused herself, and pretending mild reproof began, "Now, Tommy, you're going wooden on those hymns. For a change you'd better practise *Sons of Liberty.* Your Aunt Louise will want to hear it, anyway."

There was a fine swing and vigour in this piece, but it was hard. Hard because it was so alive, so full of youth and head-high rhythm. It was a march, and it did march. I couldn't take time to practise at the hard spots slowly till I got them right, for I had to march too. I had to let my fingers sometimes miss a note or strike one wrong. Again and again this afternoon I started carefully, resolving to count right through, the way Miss Wiggins did, and as often I sprang ahead to lead my march a moment or two all dash and fire, and then fall stumbling in the bitter dust of dissonance. My mother didn't know. She thought that speed and perseverance would eventually get me there. She tapped her foot and smiled encouragement, and gradually as the afternoon wore on began to look a little disappointed that there were to be no visitors, after all. "Run along for the cows," she said at last, "while I get supper ready for your father. There'll be nobody here, so you can slip into your overalls again."

I looked at her a moment, and then asked: "What am I going to wear to town tomorrow? I might get grease or something on the corduroys."

For while it was always my way to exploit the future, I liked to do it rationally, within the limits of the sane and probable. On my way for the cows I wanted to live the trip to town tomorrow many times, with variations, but only on the explicit understanding that tomorrow there was to be a trip to town. I have always been tethered to reality, always compelled by an unfortunate kind of probity in my nature to prefer a bare-faced disappointment to the luxury of a future I have no just claims upon.

I went to town the next day, though not till there had been a full hour's argument that paradoxically enough gave all three of us the victory. For my father had his way: I went; I had my way: I went; and in return for her consent my mother wrung a promise from him of a pair of new plush curtains for the parlour when the crop was threshed, and for me the metronome that Miss Wiggins declared was the only way I'd ever learn to keep in time on marching pieces like the *Sons of Liberty*.

It was my first trip to town alone. That was why they gave me Rock, who was old and reliable and philosophic enough to meet motorcars and the chance locomotive on an equal and even somewhat supercilious footing.

"Mind you pick somebody big and husky," said my father as he started for the field. "Go to Jenkins' store, and he'll tell you who's in town. Whoever it is, make sure he's stooked before."

"And mind it's somebody who looks like he washes himself," my mother warned, "I'm going to put clean sheets and pillow-cases on the bunkhouse bed, but not for any dirty tramp or hobo."

By the time they had both finished with me there were a great many things to mind. Besides repairs for my father's binder, I was to take two crates of eggs each containing twelve dozen eggs to Mr. Jenkins' store and in exchange have a list of groceries filled. And to make it complicated, both quantity and quality of some of the groceries were to be determined by the price of eggs. Thirty cents a dozen, for instance, and I was to ask for coffee at sixty-five cents a pound. Twenty-nine cents a dozen and coffee at fifty cents a pound. Twenty-eight and no oranges. Thirty-one and bigger oranges. It was like decimals with Miss Wiggins, or two notes in the treble against three in the bass. For my father a tin of special blend tobacco, and my mother not to know. For my mother a box of face powder at the drugstore, and my father not to know. Twenty-five cents from my father on the side for ice-cream and licorice. Thirty-five from my mother for my dinner at the Chinese restaurant. And warnings, of course, to take good care of Rock, speak politely to Mr. Jenkins, and see that I didn't get machine oil on my corduroys.

It was three hours to town with Rock, but I don't remember them. I remember nothing but a smug satisfaction with myself, an exhilarating conviction of importance and maturity—and that only by contrast with the sudden sag to embarrassed insignificance when finally old Rock and I drove up to Jenkins' store.

For a farm boy is like that. Alone with himself and his horse he cuts a fine figure. He is the measure of the universe. He foresees a great many encounters with life, and in them all acquits himself a little more than creditably. He is fearless, resourceful, a bit of a brag. His horse never contradicts.

But in town it is different. There are eyes here, critical, that pierce with a single glance the little bubble of his self-importance, and leave him dwindled smaller even than his normal size. It always happens that way. They are so superbly poised and sophisticated, these strangers, so completely masters of their situation as they loll in doorways and go sauntering up and down Main Street. Instantly he yields to them his place as measure of the universe, especially if he is a small boy wearing squeaky corduroys, especially if he has a worldly-wise old horse like Rock, one that knows his Main Streets, and will take them in nothing but his own slow philosophic stride.

We arrived all right. Mr. Jenkins was a little man with a freckled bald head, and when I carried in my two crates of eggs, one in each hand, and my legs bowed a bit, he said curtly, "Well, can't you set them down? My boy's delivering, and I can't take time to count them now myself."

"They don't need counting," I said politely. "Each layer holds two dozen, and each crate holds six layers. I was there. I saw my mother put them in."

At this a tall, slick-haired young man in yellow shoes who had been standing by the window turned around and said, "That's telling you, Jenkins—he was there." Nettled and glowering, Jenkins himself came round the counter and repeated, "So you were there, were you? Smart youngster! What did you say was your name?"

Nettled in turn to preciseness I answered, "I haven't yet. It's Thomas Dickson and my father's David Dickson, eight miles north of here. He wants a man to stook and was too busy to come himself."

He nodded, unimpressed, and then putting out his hand said, "Where's your list? Your mother gave you one, I hope?"

I said she had and he glowered again. "Then let's have it and come back in half an hour. Whether you were there or not, I'm going to count your eggs. How do I know that half of them aren't smashed?"

"That's right," agreed the young man, sauntering to the door and looking at Rock. "They've likely been bouncing along at a merry clip. You're quite sure, Buddy, that you didn't have a runaway?"

Ignoring the impertinence I staved off Jenkins. "The list, you see, has to be explained. I'd rather wait and tell you about it later on."

He teetered a moment on his heels and toes, then tried again. "I can read too. I make up orders every day. Just go away for a while—look for your man—anything."

"It wouldn't do," I persisted. "The way this one's written isn't what it really means. You'd need me to explain—"

He teetered rapidly. "Show me just one thing I don't know what it means."

"Oranges," I said, "but that's only oranges if eggs are twenty-nine cents or more—and bigger oranges if they're thirty-one. You see, you'd never understand—"

So I had my way and explained it all right then and there. What with eggs at twenty-nine and a half cents a dozen and my mother out a little in her calculations, it was somewhat confusing for a while; but after arguing a lot and pulling away the paper from each other that they were figuring on, the young man and Mr. Jenkins finally had it all worked out, with mustard and soap omitted altogether, and an extra half-dozen oranges thrown in. "Vitamins," the young man overruled me, "they make you grow"—and then with a nod towards an open biscuit box invited me to help myself.

I took a small one, and started up Rock again. It was nearly one o'clock now, so in anticipation of his noonday quart of oats he trotted off, a little more briskly, for the farmers' hitching-rail beside the lumber-yard. This was the quiet end of town. The air drowsed redolent of pine and tamarack, and resin simmering slowly in the sun. I poured out the oats and waited till he had finished. After the way the town had treated me it was comforting and peaceful to stand with my fingers in his mane, hearing him munch. It brought me a sense of place again in life. It made me feel almost as important as before. But when he finished and there was my own dinner to be thought about I found myself more of an alien in the town than ever, and felt the way to the little Chinese restaurant doubly hard. For Rock was older than I. Older and wiser, with a better understanding of important things. His philosophy included the relishing of oats even within a stone's throw of sophisticated Main Street. Mine was less mature.

I went, however, but I didn't have dinner. Perhaps it was my stomach, all puckered and tense with nervousness. Perhaps it was the restaurant itself, the pyramids of oranges in the window and the dark green rubber plant with the tropical-looking leaves, the indolent little Chinaman behind the counter and the dusky smell of last night's cigarettes that to my prairie nostrils was the orient itself, the exotic atmosphere about it all with which a meal of meat and vegetables and pie would have somehow simply jarred. I climbed onto a stool and ordered an ice-cream soda.

A few stools away there was a young man sitting. I kept watching him and wondering.

He was well-dressed, a nonchalance about his clothes that distinguished him from anyone I had ever seen, and yet at the same time it was a shabby suit, with shiny elbows and threadbare cuffs. His hands were slender, almost a girl's hands, yet vaguely with their shapely quietness they troubled me, because, however slender and smooth, they were yet hands to be reckoned with, strong with a strength that was different from the rugged labour-strength I knew.

He smoked a cigarette, and blew rings towards the window.

Different from the farmer boys I knew, yet different also from the young man with the yellow shoes in Jenkins' store. Staring out at it through the restaurant window he was as far away from Main Street as was I with plodding old Rock and my squeaky corduroys. I presumed for a minute or two an imaginary companionship. I finished my soda, and to be with him a little longer ordered lemonade. It was strangely important to be with him, to prolong a while this companionship. I hadn't the slightest hope of his noticing me, nor the slightest intention of obtruding myself. I just wanted to be there, to be assured by something I had never encountered before, to store it up for the three hours home with old Rock.

Then a big, unshaven man came in, and slouching onto the stool beside me said, "They tell me across the street you're looking for a couple of hands. What's your old man pay this year?"

"My father," I corrected him, "doesn't want a couple of men. He just wants one."

"I've got a pal," he insisted, "and we always go together."

I didn't like him. I couldn't help making contrasts with the cool, trim quietness of the young man sitting farther along. "What do you say?" he said as I sat silent, thrusting his stubby chin out almost over my lemonade. "We're ready any time."

"It's just one man my father wants," I said aloofly, drinking off my lemonade with a flourish to let him see I meant it. "And if you'll excuse me now—I've got to look for somebody else."

"What about this?" he intercepted me, and doubling up his arm displayed a hump of muscle that made me, if not more inclined to him, at least a little more deferential. "My pal's got plenty, too. We'll set up two stooks any day for anybody else's one."

"Not both," I edged away from him. "I'm sorry—you just wouldn't do."

He shook his head contemptuously. "Some farmer—just one man to stook."

"My father's a good farmer," I answered stoutly, rallying to the family honour less for its own sake than for what the young man on the other stool might think of us. "And he doesn't need just one man to stook. He's got three already. That's plenty other years, but this year the crop's so big he needs another. So there!"

"I can just see the place," he said, slouching to his feet and starting towards the door. "An acre or two of potatoes and a couple of dozen hens."

I glared after him a minute, then climbed back onto the stool and ordered another soda. The young man was watching me now in the big mirror behind the counter, and when I glanced up and met his eyes he gave a slow, half-smiling little nod of approval. And out of all proportion to anything it could mean, his nod encouraged me. I didn't flinch or fidget as I would have done had it been the young man with the yellow shoes watching me, and I didn't stammer over the confession that his amusement and appraisal somehow forced from me. "We haven't three men—just my father—but I'm to take one home today. The wheat's ripening fast this year and shelling, so he can't do it all himself."

He nodded again and then after a minute asked quietly, "What about me? Would I do?"

I turned on the stool and stared at him.

"I need a job, and if it's any recommendation there's only one of me."

"You don't understand," I started to explain, afraid to believe that perhaps he really did. "It's to stook. You have to be in the field by seven o'clock and there's only a bunkhouse to sleep in—a granary with a bed in it—"

"I know—that's about what I expect." He drummed his fingers a minute, then twisted his lips into a kind of half-hearted smile and went on, "They tell me a little toughening up is what I need. Outdoors, and plenty of good hard work—so I'll be like the fellow that just went out."

The wrong hands: white slender fingers, I knew they'd never do—but catching the twisted smile again I pushed away my soda and said quickly, "Then we'd better start right away. It's three hours home, and I've still some places to go. But you can get in the buggy now, and we'll drive around together."

We did. I wanted it that way, the two of us, to settle scores with Main Street. I wanted to capture some of old Rock's disdain and unconcern; I wanted to know what it felt like to take young men with yellow shoes in my stride, to be preoccupied, to forget them the moment that we separated. And I did. "My name's Philip," the stranger said as we drove from Jenkins' to the drugstore. "Philip Coleman—usually just Phil," and companionably I responded, "Mine's Tommy Dickson. For the last year, though, my father says I'm getting big and should be called just Tom."

That was what mattered now, the two of us there, and not the town at all. "Do you drive yourself all the time?" he asked, and nonchalant and off-hand I answered, "You don't really have to drive old Rock. He just goes, anyway. Wait till you see my chestnut three-year-old. Clipper I call him. Tonight after supper if you like you can take him for a ride."

But since he'd never learned to ride at all he thought Rock would do better for a start, and then we drove back to the restaurant for his cornet and valise.

"Is it something to play?" I asked as we cleared the town. "Something like a bugle?"

He picked up the black leather case from the floor of the buggy and held it on his knee. "Something like that. Once I played a bugle too. A cornet's better, though."

"And you mean you can play the cornet?"

He nodded. "I play in a band. At least I did play in a band. Perhaps if I get along all right with the stooking I will again some time."

It was later that I pondered this, how stooking for my father could have anything to do with going back to play in a band. At the moment I confided, "I've never heard a cornet—never even seen one. I suppose you still play it sometimes—I mean at night, when you've finished stooking."

Instead of answering directly he said, "That means you've never heard a band either." There was surprise in his voice, almost incredulity, but it was kindly. Somehow I didn't feel ashamed because I had lived all my eleven years on a prairie farm, and knew nothing more than Miss Wiggins and my Aunt Louise's gramophone. He went on, "I was younger than you are now when I started playing in a band. Then I was with an orchestra a while—then with the band again. It's all I've done ever since."

It made me feel lonely for a while, isolated from the things in life that mattered, but, brightening presently, I asked, "Do you know a piece called *Sons of Liberty?* Four flats in four-four time?"

He thought hard a minute, and then shook his head. "I'm afraid I don't—not by name anyway. Could you whistle a bit of it?"

I whistled two pages, but still he shook his head. "A nice tune, though," he conceded. "Where did you learn it?"

"I haven't yet," I explained. "Not properly, I mean. It's been my lesson for the last two weeks, but I can't keep up to it."

He seemed interested, so I went on and told him about my lessons and Miss Wiggins, and how later on they were going to buy me a metronome so that when I played a piece I wouldn't always be running away with it, "Especially a march. It keeps pulling you along the way it really ought to go until you're all mixed up and have to start at the beginning again. I know I'd do better if I didn't feel that way, and could keep slow and steady like Miss Wiggins."

But he said quickly, "No, that's the right way to feel—you've just got to learn to harness it. It's like old Rock here and Clipper. The way you are, you're Clipper. But if you weren't that way, if you didn't get excited and wanted to run sometimes, you'd just be Rock. You see? Rock's easier to handle than Clipper, but at his best he's a sleepy old plow-horse. Clipper's harder to handle—he may even cost you some tumbles. But finally get him broken in and you've got a horse that amounts to something. You wouldn't trade him for a dozen like Rock."

It was a good enough illustration, but it slandered Rock. And he was listening. I know—because even though like me he had never heard a cornet before, he had experience enough to accept it at least with tact and manners.

For we hadn't gone much farther when Philip, noticing the way I kept watching the case that was still on his knee, undid the clasps and took the cornet out. It was a very lovely cornet, shapely and eloquent, gleaming in the August sun like pure and mellow gold. I couldn't restrain myself. I said, "Play it—play it now—just a little bit to let me hear." And in response, smiling at my earnestness, he raised it to his lips.

But there was only one note—only one fragment of a note—and then away went Rock. I'd never have believed he had it in him. With a snort and plunge he was off the road and into the ditch—then out of the ditch again and off at a breakneck gallop across the prairie. There were stones and badger holes, and he spared us none of them. The egg-crates full of groceries bounced out, then the tobacco, then my mother's face powder. "Whoa, Rock!" I cried, "Whoa, Rock!" but in the rattle and whir of wheels I don't suppose he even heard. Philip couldn't help much because he had his cornet to hang on to. I tried to tug on the reins, but at such a rate across the prairie it took me all my time to keep from following the groceries. He was a big horse, Rock, and once under way had to run himself out. Or he may have thought that if he gave us a thorough shaking-up we would be too subdued when it was over to feel like taking him seriously to task. Anyway, that was how it worked out. All I dared to do was run round to pat his sweaty neck and say, "Good Rock, good Rock—nobody's going to hurt you."

Besides there were the groceries to think about, and my mother's box of face powder. And his pride and reputation at stake, Rock had made it a runaway worthy of the horse he really was. We found the powder smashed open and one of the egg-crates cracked. Several of the oranges had rolled down a badger hole, and couldn't be recovered. We spent nearly ten minutes sifting raisins through our fingers, and still they felt a little gritty. "There were extra oranges," I tried to encourage Philip, "and I've seen my mother wash her raisins." He looked at me dubiously, and for a few minutes longer worked away trying to mend the egg-crate.

We were silent for the rest of the way home. We thought a great deal about each other, but asked no questions. Even though it was safely away in its case again I could still feel the cornet's presence as if it were a living thing. Somehow its gold and shapeliness persisted, transfiguring the day, quickening the dusty harvest fields to a gleam and lustre like its own. And I felt assured, involved. Suddenly there was a force in life, a current, an inevitability, carrying me along too. The questions they would ask when I reached home—the difficulties in making them understand that faithful old Rock had really run away—none of it now seemed to matter. This stranger with the white thin hands, this gleaming cornet that as yet I hadn't even heard, intimately and enduringly now they were my possessions.

When we reached home my mother was civil and no more. "Put your things in the bunkhouse," she said, "and then wash here. Supper'll be ready in about an hour."

It was an uncomfortable meal. My father and my mother kept looking at Philip and exchanging glances. I told them about the cornet and the runaway, and they listened stonily. "We've never had a harvest-hand before that was a musician too," my mother said in a somewhat thin voice. "I suppose, though, you do know how to stook?"

I was watching Philip desperately and for my sake he lied, "Yes, I stooked last year. I may have a blister or two by this time tomorrow, but my hands will toughen up."

"You don't as a rule do farm work?" my father asked.

And Philip said, "No, not as a rule."

There was an awkward silence, so I tried to champion him. "He plays his cornet in a band. Ever since he was my age—that's what he does."

Glances were exchanged again. The silence continued.

I had been half-intending to suggest that Philip bring his cornet into the house to play it for us, I perhaps playing with him on the piano, but the parlour with its genteel plushiness was a room from which all were excluded but the equally genteel—visitors like Miss Wiggins and the minister—and gradually as the meal progressed I came to understand that Philip and his cornet, so far as my mother was concerned, had failed to qualify.

So I said nothing when he finished his supper, and let him go back to the bunkhouse alone. "Didn't I say to have Jenkins pick him out?" my father stormed as soon as he had gone. "Didn't I say somebody big and strong?"

"He's tall," I countered, "and there wasn't anybody else except two men, and it was the only way they'd come."

"You mean you didn't want anybody else. A cornet player! Fine stooks he'll set up." And then, turning to my mother, "It's your fault—you and your nonsense about music lessons. If you'd listen to me sometimes, and try to make a man of him."

"I do listen to you," she answered quickly. "It's because I've had to listen to you now for thirteen years that I'm trying to make a different man of him. If you'd go to town yourself instead of keeping him out of school—and do your work in six days a week like decent people. I told you yesterday that in the long run it would cost you dear."

I slipped away and left them. The chores at the stable took me nearly an hour; and then, instead of returning to the house, I went over to see Philip. It was dark now, and there was a smoky lantern lit. He sat on the only chair, and in a hospitable silence motioned me to the bed. At once he ignored and accepted me. It was as if we had always known each other and long outgrown the need of conversation. He smoked, and blew rings towards the open door where the warm fall night encroached. I waited, eager, afraid lest they call me to the house, yet knowing that I must wait. Gradually the flame in the lantern smoked the glass till scarcely his face was left visible. I sat tense, expectant, wondering who he was, where he came from, why he should be here to do my father's stooking.

There were no answers, but presently he reached for his cornet. In the dim, soft darkness I could see it glow and quicken. And I remember still what a long and fearful moment it was, crouched and steeling myself, waiting for him to begin.

And I was right: when they came the notes were piercing, golden as the cornet itself, and they gave life expanse that it had never known before. They floated up against the night, and each for a moment hung there clear and visible. Sometimes they mounted poignant and sheer. Sometimes they soared and then, like a bird alighting, fell and brushed earth again.

It was *To the Evening Star*. He finished it and told me. He told me the names of all the other pieces that he played: an *Ave Maria*, *Song of India*, a serenade—all bright through the dark like slow, suspended lightning, chilled sometimes with a glimpse of the unknown. Only for Philip there I could not have endured it. With my senses I clung hard to him—the acrid smell of his cigarettes, the tilted profile daubed with smoky light.

Then abruptly he stood up, as if understanding, and said, "Now we'd better have a march, Tom—to bring us back where we belong. A cornet can be good fun, too, you know. Listen to this one and tell me."

He stood erect, head thrown back exactly like a picture in my reader of a bugler boy, and the notes came flashing gallant through the night until the two of us went swinging along in step with them a hundred thousand strong. For this was another march that did march. It marched us miles. It made the feet eager and the heart brave. It said that life was worth the living and bright as morning shone ahead to show the way.

When he had finished and put the cornet away I said, "There's a field right behind the house that my father started cutting this afternoon. If you like we'll go over now for a few minutes and I'll show you how to stook.... You see, if you set your sheaves on top of the stubble they'll be over again in half an hour. That's how everybody does at first but it's wrong. You've got to push the butts down hard, right to the ground—like this, so they bind with the stubble. At a good slant, see, but not too much. So they'll stand the wind and still shed water if it rains."

It was too dark for him to see much, but he listened hard and finally succeeded in putting up a stook or two that to my touch seemed firm enough. Then my mother called, and I had to slip away fast so that she would think I was coming from the bunkhouse. "I hope he stooks as well as he plays," she said when I went in. "Just the same, you should have done as your father told you, and picked a likelier man to see us through the fall."

My father came in from the stable then, and he, too, had been listening. With a wondering, half-incredulous little movement of his head he made acknowledgement.

"Didn't I tell you he could?" I burst out, encouraged to indulge my pride in Philip. "Didn't I tell you he could play?" But with sudden anger in his voice he answered, "And what if he can! It's a man to stook I want. Just look at the hands on him. I don't think he's ever seen a farm before."

It was helplessness, though, not anger. Helplessness to escape his wheat when wheat was not enough, when something more than wheat had just revealed itself. Long after they were both asleep I remembered, and with a sharp foreboding that we might have to find another man, tried desperately to sleep myself. "Because if I'm up in good time," I rallied all my faith in life, "I'll be able to go to the field with him and at least make sure he's started right. And he'll maybe do. I'll ride down after school and help till supper time. My father's reasonable."

Only in such circumstances, of course, and after such a day, I couldn't sleep till nearly morning, with the result that when at last my mother wakened me there was barely time to dress and ride to school. But of the day I spent there I remember nothing. Nothing except the midriff clutch of dread that made it a long day—nothing, till straddling Clipper at four again, I galloped him straight to the far end of the farm where Philip that morning had started to work.

Only Philip, of course, wasn't there. I think I knew—I think it was what all day I had been expecting. I pulled Clipper up short and sat staring at the stooks. Three or four acres of them—crooked and dejected as if he had never heard about pushing the butts down hard into the stubble. I sat and stared till Clipper himself swung round and started for home. He wanted to run, but because there was nothing left now but the half-mile ahead of us, I held him to a walk. Just to prolong a little the possibility that I had misunderstood things. To wonder within the limits of the sane and probable if tonight he would play his cornet again.

When I reached the house my father was already there, eating an early supper. "I'm taking him back to town," he said quietly. "He tried hard enough—he's just not used to it. The sun was hot today; he lasted till about noon. We're starting in a few minutes, so you'd better go out and see him."

He looked older now, stretched out limp on the bed, his face haggard. I tiptoed close to him anxiously, afraid to speak. He pulled his mouth sidewise in a smile at my concern, then motioned me to sit down. "Sorry I didn't do better," he said. "I'll have to come back another year and have another lesson."

I clenched my hands and clung hard to this promise that I knew he couldn't keep. I wanted to rebel against what was happening, against the clumsiness and crudity of life, but instead I stood quiet a moment, almost passive, then wheeled away and carried out his cornet to the buggy. My mother was already there, with a box of lunch and some ointment for his sunburn. She said she was sorry things had turned out this way, and thanking her politely he said that he was sorry too. My father looked uncomfortable, feeling, no doubt, that we were all unjustly blaming everything on him. It's like that on a farm. You always have to put the harvest first.

And that's all there is to tell. He waved going through the gate; I never saw him again. We watched the buggy down the road to the first turn, then with a quick resentment in her voice my mother said, "Didn't I say that the little he gained would in the long run cost him dear? Next time he'll maybe listen to me—and remember the Sabbath Day."

What exactly she was thinking I never knew. Perhaps of the crop and the whole day's stooking lost. Perhaps of the stranger who had come with his cornet for a day, and then as meaninglessly gone again. For she had been listening, too, and she may have understood. A harvest, however lean, is certain every year; but a cornet at night is golden only once.

Scrub Oak

I saw an oak once less than three feet high,
A prairie oak, full grown. It grew in sand
With others of its kind, all taller but
None tall. I've known oaks in a kindlier land
Attain a height and girth and a supply
Of dignity; but these could barely jut
Their jagged arms (they had no trunks) above
The ground. Eking a hard existence, there
They stood, defiant, grim, but still alive.

You'd wonder why these oaks were growing where
They couldn't grow. Some kindly, pleasant grove
Would suit them better, where they'd live and thrive
And prosper as they ought.

Life has a way
Of doing things we don't expect her to:
I don't know why these oak trees should have grown
There where they did in that unlikely view,
Or why persisted in their stubborn sway
Against what odds, unlovely and alone.

Cottonwood

It's strange how you get used to things. You take
That cottonwood that grew there in the yard
Beside my window. I had lived alone,
Here on the farm, for years. The life was hard,
But never lonely-like. I felt no ache
Of loneliness until that tree was gone.

I never mind I paid much heed to it
Until the lightning struck, splitting it clean
Down through the middle of the trunk; and then
I missed the sighing whisper that had been
A voice against my loneliness. It split
A friendship I can never know again.

CAROL SHIELDS

Flitting Behavior

Some of Meershank's wittiest writing was done during his wife's final illness.

"Mortality," he whispered each morning to give himself comfort, "puts acid in the wine." Other times he said, as he peered into the bathroom mirror, "Mortality puts strychnine in the candy floss. It puts bite in the byte." Then he groaned aloud—but only once—and got straight back to work.

His novel of this period, *Malaprop In Disneyfield*, was said to have been cranked out of the word processor between invalid trays and bedpans. In truth, he wept as he set down his outrageous puns and contretemps. The pages mounted, 200, 300. The bulk taunted him, and meanwhile his wife, Louise, lingered, her skin growing as transparent as human skin can be without disintegrating. A curious odor, bitter and yellow, stole over the sickroom. Meershank had heard of the odor which preceded death; now he breathed it daily.

It was for this odor, more than anything else, that he pitied her, she who'd busied herself all her life warding off evil smells with scented candles and aerosol room fresheners. Since a young woman she'd had the habit of sweetening her bureau drawers, and his too, with sprigs of dried lavender, and carrying always in her handbag and traveling case tiny stitched sachets of herbs. He had sometimes wondered where she found these anachronistic sachets; who in the modern industrial world produced such frivolities?—the Bulgarians maybe, or the Peruvians, frantic for hard currency.

Toward the end of Louise's illness he had a surprise visit from his editor, a vigorous, leggy woman of forty who drove up from Toronto to see how the new manuscript was coming along. She came stepping from her car one Monday afternoon in a white linen jumpsuit. Bending slightly, she kissed Meershank on both cheeks and cried out, "But this is extraordinary! That you can even think of work at a time like this."

Meershank pronounced for her his bite-in-the-byte aperçu, very nearly choking with shame.

He was fond of his editor—her name was Maybelle Spritz—but declined to invite her into his wife's bedroom, though the two women knew and liked each other. "She's not strong enough for visitors," he said, knowing it was the smell of the room he guarded her from, his poor Louise's last corner of pride. "Maybe later."

He and Maybelle sat drinking coffee on the veranda most of the afternoon. The weather all week had been splendid. Birds sang in the branches of Meershank's trees, and sunlight flooded the long triangle of Meershank's side lawn. Maybelle, reading slowly as always, turned over the manuscript pages. Her nails were long and vivid. She held a pencil straight up in her hand, and at least once every three minutes or so she let loose a bright snort of laughter which Meershank welcomed like a man famished. He watched her braided loop of auburn hair and observed how the light burned on the tips of her heavy silver earrings. There was a bony hollow at the base of her neck that deepened, suddenly, each time another snort was gathering. Later, at five o'clock, checking his watch, he offered gin and tonic. For Louise upstairs he carried cream of celery soup, weak tea and an injection for her hip, which the visiting nurse had taught him to administer.

"Are you feeling lonely?" his wife asked him, turning on one side and readying herself for the needle. She imagined, rightly, that he missed her chatter, that her long days spent in drugged sleep were a deprivation. Every day she asked the same question, plunging him directly into blocky silence. Yes, he was lonely. No, he was not lonely. Which would please her more? He kept his hand on her discolored hip and mumbled the news—testing it—that Maybelle Spritz was thinking of coming for a visit.

She opened her eyes and managed a smile as he rearranged the pillows. He had a system: one pillow under each knee, one at the small of her back and two to support her shoulders. The air in the room was suffocating. He asked again, as he did every day, if he might open a window. No, she said, as she always did; it was too cold. She seemed convinced that spring had not arrived in its usual way, she who'd always been so reasonable.

Downstairs Maybelle stood in the kitchen drinking a second gin and tonic and heating up a noodle pudding she had brought along. She had occasionally been a dinner guest in Meershank's house, but had never before penetrated the kitchen. She set a little table on the veranda. There was a breeze, enough to keep the mosquitoes away for a bit. Knives and forks; she discovered them easily in the first drawer she opened. The thick white dinner plates she found stacked on a shelf over the sink. There were paper napkins of a most ordinary sort in a cupboard. As she moved about,she marveled at the domesticity of the famous, how simple things appeared when regarded close up, like picking up an immense orange and finding it all thick hide on a tiny fruit. She wondered if Meershank would ask her to spend the night.

They had only once before shared a bed, and that had been during the awful week after Louise's illness had been diagnosed.

The expression *terminal*, when the doctor first pronounced it, had struck Meershank with a comic bounce, this after a lifetime of pursuing puns for a living. His scavenger self immediately pictured a ghostly airline terminal in which scurrying men and women trotted briskly to and fro in hospital gowns.

The word *terminal* had floated out of the young doctor's wide pink face; it was twice repeated, until Meershank collected himself and responded with a polite nod. Then he put back his head, counted the ceiling tiles—twelve times fourteen—and decided on the spot that his wife must not be told.

The specialist laced clean hands across flannel knees and pressed for honest disclosure; there were new ways of telling people that they were about to die; he himself had attended a recent symposium in Boston and would take personal responsibility...

No. Meershank held up his hand. This was nonsense. Why did people insist that honesty was the only way of coping with truth? He knew his wife. After thirty-five years of marriage he knew his wife. She must be brought home from the hospital and encouraged to believe that she would recover. Rest, medication, country air— they would work their healing magic. Louise could always, almost always, be persuaded to follow a reasonable course.

The following day, having signed the release papers and made the arrangements to have his wife moved, Meershank, until then a faithful husband, took his editor, Maybelle Spritz, to a downtown hotel and made plodding love to her, afterward begging pardon for his age, his grief, and his fury at the fresh-faced specialist who, concluding their interview, had produced one of Meershank's books, *Walloping Westward*, and begged the favor of an inscription. Meershank coldly took out a pen and signed his name. He reminded himself that the Persians had routinely put to death the bearer of bad news.

Home again, with Louise installed in the big front bedroom, he resumed work. His word processor hummed like a hornet from nine to five and the pages flew incriminatingly out of the printer. During the day his brain burned like a lightbulb screwed crookedly into a socket. At night he slept deeply. He wondered if he were acquiring a reputation for stoicism, that contemptible trait! Friends stopped by with gifts of food or flowers. The flowers he carried up to Louise's bedroom where they soon drooped and died, and the food he threw in the garbage. Coffee cakes, almond braids, banana loaves—his appetite had vanished.

"Eat," Maybelle commanded, loading his plate.

He loved noodle pudding, and wondered how Maybelle knew. "It's in your second novel," she reminded him. "*Snow Soup and*

Won Ton Drift. Remember? Wentzel goes into the cafe at Cannes and demands that—"

"I remember, I remember," Meershank held up a hand. (He was always holding up a hand nowadays, resisting information.) He had a second helping, injesting starch and sweetness. This was hardly fitting behavior for a grieving husband. He felt Maybelle's eyes on him. "I shoulda brought more," she said, sounding for a minute like a girl from Cookston Corners, which she was. "I said to myself, he'll be starving himself."

For dessert she rummaged in the refrigerator and found two peaches. Louise would have peeled them and arranged the slices in a cut glass bowl. Meershank and Maybelle sat eating them out of their hands. He thought to himself: this is like the last day of the world.

"Ripe," Maybelle pronounced. There was a droplet of juice on her chin, which she brushed away with the back of her hand. Meershank observed that her eyes looked tired, but perhaps it was only the eye shadow she wore. What was the purpose of eye shadow, he wondered. He had never known and couldn't begin to imagine.

A character in his first book, *Swallowing Hole*, had asked this question aloud to another character, who happened to be his wife. What was her name? Phyllis? Yes, Phyllis of the phyllo pastry and philandering nights. "Why do you smudge your gorgeous green eyes with gook?" he, the cuckolded husband, had asked. And what had the fair Phyllis replied? Something arch, something unpardonable. Something enclosing a phallic pun. He had forgotten, and for that he blessed the twisted god of age. His early books with their low-altitude gag lines embarrassed him and he tried hard to forget he had once been the idiot who wrote them.

Maybelle, on the other hand, knew his oeuvre with depressing thoroughness and could quote chapter and verse. Well, that was the function of an editor, he supposed. A reasonable man would be grateful for such attention. She was a good girl. He wished she'd find a husband so he would feel less often that she'd taken the veil on his account. But at least she didn't expect him to converse with wit. Like all the others, she'd bought wholesale the myth of the sad jester.

It was a myth that he himself regarded with profound skepticism. He'd read the requisite scholarly articles, of course, and had even, hypocrite that he was, written one or two himself. Humor is a pocket pulled inside out; humor is an anguished face dumped upside down; humor is the refuge of the grunting cynic, the eros of the deprived lover, the breakfast of the starving clown. Some of these cheap theories he'd actually peddled aloud to the graduating class at Trent a year ago, and his remarks had been applauded lustily. (How much better to lust applaudingly, he'd cackled, sniggered, snorted inside his wicked head.)

He suspected that these theories were leapt upon for their simplicity, their symmetry, their neat-as-a-pin ironic shimmer. They were touted by those so facile they were unable to see how rich with ragged comedy the world really was. But Meershank knew, he knew! Was it not divinely comic that only yesterday he'd received a telephone solicitation from the Jackson Point Cancer Fund? Wasn't it also comic that the specter of his wife's death should fill him with a wobbly lust for his broad-busted, perfume-wafting, forty-year-old editor? For that matter, wasn't it superbly comic that a man widely known as a professional misogynist had remained happily married to one woman for thirty-five years? (Life throws these kinky curves a little too often, Meershank had observed, and the only thing to do was open your fool mouth and guffaw.)

At nine he checked once again on his wife, who was sleeping quietly. If she woke later, a second injection was permitted. He carried a bottle of brandy out on to the veranda. One for the road, he asked Maybelle with his eyebrows. Why not, she said with a lift of her shoulders. Her upper lip went stiff as a ledge in the moonlight and he shuddered to think he was about to kiss her. The moon tonight was bloated and white, as fretful as a face. Everywhere there was the smell of mock-orange blossoms which had bloomed early this year and in absurd profusion. Crickets ticked in the grass, like fools, like drunkards. Meershank lifted his glass. The brandy burned his throat and made him retreat for an instant, but Maybelle became attenuated, lively, sharp of phrase, amusing. He laughed aloud for the first time in a week, wondering if the world would crack down the middle.

It did. Or seemed to. A loud overhead popping noise like the cracking of whips made him jump. Maybelle slammed down her glass and stared. All around them the sky flashed white, then pink, then filled with rat-a-tat-tat fountains and sparks and towering plumes.

"Jesus," Maybelle said. "Victoria Day. I almost forgot."

"I did forget," Meershank said. "I never once thought."

A rocket whined and popped, made ropy arcs across the sky, burst into petals, leaving first one, then a dozen blazing trails. It was suddenly daylight, fierce, then faded, then instantly replaced by a volley of cracking gunpowder and new showers of brilliance.

The explosions, star-shaped, convulsive, leaping one out of the other, made Meershank think of the chains of malignant cells igniting in his wife's body.

He set down his brandy, excused himself, and hurried upstairs.

Meershank, marrying Louise Lovell in 1949, had felt himself rubbing bellies for the first time with the exotic. He, a Chicago Jew, the son of a bond salesman, had fallen in love with a gentile, a Canadian, a fair-haired girl of twenty who had been gently reared in the Ottawa Valley by parents who lived quietly in a limestone house that was a hundred years old. It faced on the river. There was a rose garden crisscrossed by gravel paths and surrounded by a pale-pink brick wall. Oh, how silently those two parents had moved about in their large square rooms, in winter wrapping themselves in shawls, sitting before pots of raspberry-leaf tea and making their good-natured remarks about the weather, the books they were forever in the middle of, the tiny thunder of politics that flickered from their newspaper, always one-day-old.

The mother of Louise possessed a calm brow of marble. The

father had small blue eyes and hard cheeks. He was the author of a history of the Canadian Navy. It was, he told Meershank, the *official* history. Meershank was given a signed copy. And he was given, too, with very little noise or trouble, the hand of Louise in marriage. He had been stunned. Effortlessly, it seemed, he'd won from them their beloved only daughter, a girl of soft hips and blond hair done roundly in a pageboy.

"What exactly do you do?" they only once asked. He worked as a correspondent for a newspaper, he explained. (He did not use the word *journalist*.) And he hoped one day to write a book. ("Ah! A book ! Splendid!")

The wedding was in the month of June and was held in the garden. Meershank's relatives did not trouble to travel all the way up from Chicago. The wedding breakfast was served out-of-doors, and the health of the young couple—Meershank at twenty-seven was already starting to bald—was toasted with a non-alcoholic fruit punch. The family was abstemious; the tradition went back several generations; alcohol, tobacco, caffeine—there wasn't a trace of these poisons in the bloodstream of Meershank's virgin bride. He looked at her smooth, pale arms—and eventually, when legally married, at her smooth pale breasts—and felt he'd been singularly, and comically, blessed.

There is a character, Virgie Allgood, in Meershank's book, *Sailing to Saskatchewan*, who might be said to resemble Louise. In the book, Virgie is an eater of whole grains and leafy vegetables. Martyrlike, she eschews French fries, doughnuts and liver dumplings, yet her body is host to disease after disease. Fortified milk fails. Pure air fails. And just when the life is about to go out of her, the final chapter, a new doctor rides into town on a motorbike and saves her by prescribing a diet of martinis and cheesecakes.

There is something of Louise, too, in the mother in Meershank's tour-de-force, *Continuous Purring*. She is a woman who cannot understand the simplest joke. Riddles on cereal boxes have to be laboriously explained. Puns strike her as being untidy scraps to be swept up in a dustpan. She thinks a double entendre is a potent new drink. She is congenitally immune to metaphor (the root of all comedy, Meershank believes) and on the day her husband is appointed to the Peevish Chair of Midbrow Humor, she sends for the upholsterer.

When *Encounter* did its full length profile on Meershank in 1981, it erred by stating that Louise Lovell Meershank had never read her husband's books. The truth is she not only had read them, but before the birth of the word processor she typed them, collated the pages, corrected their virulent misspelling, redistributed semicolons and commas with the aplomb of a goddess, and tactfully weeded out at least half of Meershank's compulsive exclamation points. She corresponded with publishers, arranged for foreign rights, dealt with book clubs and with autograph seekers, and she always—less and less frequently of course—trimmed her husband's fluffy wreath of hair with a pair of silver-handled scissors.

She read Meershank's manuscripts with a delicious (to Meershank) frown on her wide pale brow—more and more she'd grown to resemble her mother. She turned over the pages with a delicate hand as though they possessed the same scholarly sheen as her father's *Official History of the Canadian Navy*. She read them not once, but several times, catching a kind of overflow of observance which leaked like oil and vinegar from the edges of Meershank's copious, verbal, many-leafed salads.

Her responses never marched in time with his. She was slower, and could wave aside sentimentality, saying, "Why not?—it's part of the human personality." Occasionally she said the unexpected thing, as when she described her husband's novella, *Fiend at the Water Fountain*, as being, "cool and straight up and down as a tulip."

What she actually told the journalist from *Encounter* was that she never *laughed* when reading her husband's books. For this Meershank has always respected her, valued her, adored her. She was his Canadian rose, his furry imbiber of scented tea, his smiling plum, his bread and jam, his little squirrel, his girlie-girl, his Dear Heart who promised in the garden by the river beside the limestone house in 1949 to stay at his side for ever and ever. What a joke she has played on him in the end.

She has, Meershank said to Maybelle, taken a turn for the worse. He phoned the doctor, who said he would come at once. Then he handed Maybelle a piece of paper on which two telephone numbers were written. "Please," he said. "Phone the children."

Maybelle was unprepared for this. And she had never met the children. "What should I tell them?" she asked.

"Tell them," Meershank said, and paused. "Tell them it could be sooner than we thought."

One of the daughters, Sonya, lived in London, Ontario where she was the new director of the program for women's studies. (For those who trouble to look, her mirror image can be found in Ira Chauvin, post-doc researcher in male studies, in Meershank's academic farce, *Ten Minutes to Tenure.*) Sonya did not say to Maybelle, "Who is this calling?" or "How long does she have?" She said, "I'll be there in three hours flat."

The other daughter, Angelica, ran a health-food restaurant and delicatessen with her husband, Rusty, in Montreal. They were just closing up for the night when Maybelle phoned. "I can get a plane at midnight," Angelica said in a high, sweet, shaky voice. "Tell her to wait for me."

After that Maybelle sat on a kitchen chair in the dark. She could have switched on the light, but she preferred to sit as she was and puzzle over what level of probability had landed her on the twenty-fourth of May as a visitor in a dying woman's shadowy kitchen. And that was what she was, only a visitor—she was not such a fool as to mistake a single embrace for anything other than a mutation of grief.

The tiles of the kitchen wall, after a moment, took on a greenish glow, and she began to float out of her body, a trick she had perfected during her long years of commuting between Cookston

Corners and downtown Toronto. First, she became Sonya flying down an eastbound highway, her hands suddenly younger and supple-jointed on the slippery wheel. She took the long cloverleafs effortlessly, the tires of her tough little car zinging over ramps and bridges, and the sleepy nighttime radio voices holding her steady in the middle lane.

Then, blinking once and shutting out the piny air, she was transformed into Angelica, candid, fearful, sitting tense in an aisle seat at the rear of a plane—she had her mother's smooth cheeks, her father's square chin and her own slow sliding tears. On her lap she clutched a straw bag, and every five minutes she pushed back the sleeve of her blouse and checked her wristwatch, trying to freeze its hands with her will.

Next she was the doctor—springing onto the veranda, tapping at the screen door and taking the stairs two at a time. She drifted then into the amorphous body of Louise where it was hot and damp and difficult to breathe, but where shadows reached out and curved around her head. Her hands lay surprisingly calm on the sheet—until one of them was lifted and held to Meershank's beating heart.

She felt his bewilderment and heard with his ears a long popping chain of firecrackers going off. A window in the bedroom had been opened—at last—and the scent of the mock orange blossoms reached him with a rushing blow. Everything was converging. All the warm fluids of life came sliding behind Maybelle's eyes, and she had to hold on to the sides of the kitchen chair to keep herself from disappearing.

In each of Meershank's fictions there is what the literary tribe calls a "set piece," a jewel, as it were, set in a spun-out text, or a chunk of narrative that is somehow more intense, more cohesive, more self-contained than the rest. Generally theatrical and vivid, it can be read and comprehended, even when severed from the wider story, or it can be "performed" by those writers—Meershank is not one—who like to gad about the country giving "readings."

In Meershank's recently published book, *Malaprop in Disneyfield*, the set piece has four characters sitting at dusk on a veranda discussing the final words of the recently deceased family matriarch. The sky they gaze into is a rainy mauve, and the mood is one of tenderness—but there is also a tone of urgency. Three of the four had been present when the last words were uttered, and some irrational prompting makes them want to share with the fourth what they heard—or what they *thought* they heard. Because each heard something different, and there is a descending order of coherence.

"The locked door of the room," is what one of them, a daughter, heard.

"The wok cringes in the womb," is the enigmatic phrase another swears she heard.

The bereaved husband, a blundering old fool in shirtsleeves, heard, incredibly, "The sock is out of tune."

All three witnesses turn to their listener, as lawyers to a judge. Not one of them is superstitious enough to place great importance on final words. Illness, they know, brings a rainbow of distortion, but they long, nevertheless, for interpretation.

The listening judge is an awkward but compassionate woman who would like nothing better than to bring these three fragments into unity. Inside her head she holds a pencil straight up. Her eyes are fixed on the purpling clouds.

Then it arrives. Through some unsecured back door in her imagination she comes up with "The mock orange is in bloom."

"Of course, of course," they chime, nodding and smiling at each other, and at that moment their grief shifts subtly, the first of many such shiftings they are about to undergo.

DOUGLAS SMITH

The History of Flight

for Pat and Gary Martens

We are stacking last summer's box-hives
littered with papery, tattered, dead
bees   The moon lurks
above the silvered cap of the silo
that rises out of the dusk
like a magnified cartridge

The boxes are heavy with wax
and crusted honey
I trip and drop one that shatters easily in the cold
Inside a clump of wings
and furry heads obscures the thumb-sized Queen   Now
nothing can arouse
her voluptuous thorax
dilate those commanding black pupils
or bristle the fine sexual antennae frozen with need

I plant her, like a delicate pod,
in the blossom of snow
on a fencepost

Later, the wind
will send her gently away
beyond the silo, toward the moon
that floats above this cold farm,
a ball of luminous pollen

Bird Brain

Up suddenly from the reed-green ditch,
across the flat highway,
over slack power lines glistening
like filaments
as the sunfall bronzes a field
of young sunflowers,
each slender stem curved like the neck
of a madonna

the heron wings his longwinded
neck into the distance
and dreams

Sky, be blue
blue

JACQUI SMYTH

Delusion

For some reason   you take refuge
in this country   it's still raw
buildings seem untouched   until
you're settled   then cracked stucco
and chipped paint become visible
You arrive in mid-winter
absence of heat convinces you
there is no passion   until
your face begins to burn and
numbness tranquilizes the pain
It's extreme here and deceiving too

It may be the shrinking walls
or the passing chinook that
forces you to slide along
paths of a diluted forest   When
the temperature drops   it's tempting
to lie here on the snowbank
and wait for spring   If you awaken
there is a lucidity on the smooth
highway   cleared of ice
You will go blind from the glare
of white land under a silver sun

This lack of snow and the existence
of icicles may give you strength
Bare branches on undisturbed lawns
remind you of black and white
peacock tails   in late spring
the deepest frost will surface
killing the planted seeds as they begin
to break through shells

Don't think of this land as hostile
think of yourself as naive
Like those parrots escaping from the Conservatory
shattering in mid-air   and falling
into the colored patterns of porcelain wings

WAYNE TEFS

Mints for Mrs H

In Red Rock in the days of our childhood the people who lived next door were Norwegian immigrants, a family of three. Hansen himself was a dour miner who worked as blasting foreman at the pits, smiled rarely, and never spoke. But his wife was different. We children called her Mrs H. She waved at us when we played in the back yard, she called our names over the fence in broken English and asked us into her kitchen for milk and macaroons. They were chocolate, rich and soft, like the looks Mrs H cast at her daughter, Mary. She was the same age as me but two years behind in school because, the teachers said, of her poor English. We children knew in the way of children that there was more to it than that, something to do with Mary's slurred speech, her split upper lip, her vacant stares. "She's a good girl, yes?" Mrs H asked us, and we nodded eager agreement. We liked Mary even though her mouth was twisted and she was slow at school. We were too young to realize it then but Mary was the butt of ugly town gossip. She was moody and reserved like her father, her sudden silences threatening to scuttle Mrs H's snack times of chewy macaroons which she pressed on us with glasses of ice cold milk.

Mary sat silent while we munched macaroons and Mrs H questioned us about school and muttered about vegetable gardening: she grew wonderful tomatoes, as my mother, whose family were market gardeners, said. After the snack Mrs H brought out music sheets and Mary sat at the piano and played. Just what she played, I do not know, great swooping pieces punctuated by intricate flurries where her painted nails lashed the keys in blurs and she laughed suddenly, high and loud. I rested my chin in my hands and studied the light dancing on her fingers. Sometimes Mrs H joined her for duets, then flushed, put her hand over her heart and offered us more macaroons. Embarrassed by her twisted lip, Mary retired to a corner, nodded sometimes, and burst into sudden laughter, an unusual sound, high and scratchy, like someone who'd heard laughing on the radio but didn't have much practice at it.

What was it about that playing? Mrs H was good in a determined germanic way, striking the keys like a sergeant major. But Mary! Frail, with long dark hair falling in tangles, she played with abandon, sunlight dancing in her green eyes, grown vacant as she became absorbed in the music. When she played she came out of the shadows of her fear and the ugliness cowering there. Her red nails leapt and plunged, beautiful passionate things, paired through some bizarre twist of fate with Mary's ugly mouth. I could have listened all day.

There were those who talked about Mary in whispered tones we children hadn't yet learned to understand. "Freak," some kids shouted at her on the schoolyard, "Mongoloid," and the children next door stopped going for milk and macaroons. One day in our house a neighbour who'd drunk too much sherry said Mrs H wasn't fit to be a mother. "Jezebel," she called Mrs H. Our own mother told us never to repeat that. Another evening she sat us down and made us recount the details of our afternoons at Mrs H's, and though our father puffed at his pipe and threw mother heavy glances, we continued to go for snacks and listen to Mary play.

Soon after, our father's business went bankrupt, we moved to another town, we grew up and gravitated to cities where we took jobs and studied at college. I spent many hours in movie houses, I spent many evenings at parties, some of them listening to pretty girls play, but I never saw anyone who played like Mary and after a time I rarely thought of her. I married and had children who themselves went to school. Then one day my older sister received an invitation to the school reunion and we found ourselves back among old friends and known but unfamiliar surroundings. We drank bad wine and chewed on cheap cheeses while former classmates and neighbors reminisced about this championship game and that teacher. Our school captain cornered my sister and me; he made a living from real estate and was grooming himself as the next mayor of the town.

"And what do you remember about Red Rock?" he asked. "Now that you're big city folk?"

"The beauties of small places," I said. "The quiet and all that. But also the stupidity of small towns."

"How do you mean?"

"The cruel and ugly thinking," I said. "Prejudices."

"Um," the school captain said, looking surprised. He rotated the plastic wine glass in his manicured fingers.

"What I remember," my sister said, "is the taste of macaroons." She smacked her lips.

"Chocolate," I added.

"Of course." He snorted. "Chocolate macaroons, and music, and hopeless Mrs H."

"Hopeless?"

"Oh my, yes. Hopeless. After the old man died, after that business with the girl...." He laughed and chewed on a wedge of cheese. "They say the old woman got what she deserved, keeping an idiot at home like that. Never would happen today, of course. They say she had it coming," he added, waving her away with one fat hand. "Now there's talk of a town ordinance." The aspiring mayor had more to say, but I lost the thread of the conversation, I heard instead Mrs H's broken English and the joyful tinkling of her piano, Mary sitting on the bench, the sun shining on her hair.

I left them with their wine and cheese and collected my two children who I'd brought to see their papa's home town and drove into our old neighborhood. There were more dogs than I recalled from my childhood and fewer rusty cars. The playground where we chased balls on Saturday afternoons was overgrown with tall grasses, and the trees my parents had planted were tall and leafy. My father's pines, my mother's russian olives, the elms we'd dug along the drive. Everything looked old and solid compared to the way I recalled it as a child. Everything except the Hansens'.

Grass grew waist high under the windows and through the asphalt driveway. The windows were dusty and the paint on the doors peeling. I left the children in the car reading comic books, I was going to give them mints, too, but decided to save them for later. I started down the sidewalk to the front entrance, heaved and broken through many winters of inattention. Badly in disrepair, unused. Remembering Mrs H's garden, I left the front entrance and went to the back yard. There were weeds choking the plots near the house and rusting lawnmower parts littered about the grass, but in the far corner of the yard I saw Mrs H's back, I saw her grey hair sticking out from under a soiled baseball cap. She was hoeing but evidently not intent on her task, for every few seconds she paused and stared straight ahead. When I drew near I realized she was talking to herself. She probed the air with the finger of one trembling hand. Up close there was the rank smell of sour flesh and unwashed clothing about her. I stood behind her, trying to make out what she was saying, it seemed to be the same thing over and over, but standing behind her I could not hear what.

"Good afternoon," I said, feeling ashamed of my quavering voice. "Mrs H...?"

Her back remained bent and she pawed at the ground with the hoe, an old tool with a soiled shaft. She stooped forward and I saw she was tending tomatoes, a dozen or so scrawny plants in dry and hard ground. She moved with difficulty. Between two fingers she plucked a weed and pushed it into one pocket of her denim jacket, as if saving something important. She stood again, studying the stunted plants. "Good afternoon," I repeated, much louder than before.

She turned to me. There was a hitch in her movement as if she'd suffered a hip injury, and she stood on one foot awkwardly to take me in. When she looked at me I remembered those eyes studying us as children, attentive eyes bright and blue, now glazed, and I seemed to shrink, I heard again the gay chirping of her immigrant's English. "It's me," I said, and waved my hand idiotically toward the house next door, occupied for twenty years now by strangers. "It's Arnold, Mrs H." She pawed the ground with her hoe for several moments as we stood in awkward silence. I felt the sun burning the top of my head. "Arnold. You remember? We used to come over to hear Mary play, we used to come over for macaroons before father...."

"She's a good girl, yes?" she asked. She lifted one hand into the air and then let it fall mechanically. Her fingernails were long and yellow, dirt encrusted.

"Who?" I asked. The sun beat down on me and I felt dizzy from wine and heat.

"They take her away," Mrs H said.

"Mary?" I remembered the frightened look in the girl's eyes, a look like that in Mrs H's now. I remembered Mary's silences while the rest of us children played kick the can on the schoolground, and how she retreated to corners, and the way she played the piano after we finished our snacks. Crimson nails. I thought of the taste of chocolate macaroons and how I always wanted to have just one more, the way chocolate stuck to the roof of my mouth. I also thought of the dark glances that passed between my parents, and the things the neighbors had said, the ugly unrepeatable words which I now understood and knew didn't apply to Mrs H or Mary. Freak, mongoloid, Jezebel. And then Mrs H's voice broke in on me.

"She's a good girl, yes?"

"Yes," I said. There were brown stones in the clay and I toed one with my blue-ribbed sneakers.

"They take her away." She looked at me as if I were to blame. Perhaps she hoped that I might do something about it. She lifted one hand again and the light slanted through the trees on the yellow nails. Cracked, I saw. Chipped. "She plays, my Mary, oh so nice—you would like to hear, maybe?" Her cloudy blue eyes were fixed on mine.

"I remember." I waited for her to say my name, to acknowledge there'd once been a connection between us, I flattered myself that she would remember the boy who was so moved by her dark-haired daughter.

But she didn't say anything about that. She didn't say, "Yes, I remember now, the boy who loved my macaroons, the boy who listened to my little Mary play." She didn't even say, "Ah, yes, Arnold" with the clear authority of sudden memory. What she said was, "She liked tomatoes." She looked at the plants as if for the first time and said, "She liked them."

I cleared my throat but no words would come, and I lowered my eyes. Scrawny plants swam in my sight. Sickly green. Mrs H began to scratch at the dirt, a nervous scraping, hoe clasped in fingers which once skipped over the keys with Mary's and brought chocolate macaroons on blue rimmed china. Now marked with neglect, dirt encrusted, gnarled knuckles. "They said they wouldn't," she said, "the doctors when we came." And when I didn't answer, "She's a good girl, yes, my Mary?"

I felt the ground sliding away from me. I was trembling, eyes welded to the scraping hoe.

"It's okay," a voice behind us said. It was a woman leaning on the garden fence, the way I'd seen my mother lean to laugh with Mrs H when we were children, the way Mrs H did calling us over for macaroons. "She doesn't understand you." She was a big woman, with plump arms and muscular wrists, and she tapped one thick finger on her temple. "Do you, dear?" She raised her voice. "And how are the tomatoes today? Big as oranges I bet they'll be."

"They take her away."

"Yes dear, I know."

Mrs H's eyes had not moved. She was looking at neither of us, but somewhere off beyond my shoulder. She said, "My Mary, she plays oh so nice—you would like to hear?"

"Not right now, dear. Maybe soon." The woman's eyes suddenly filled with tears and in a moment she took out a polka-dot handkerchief and blew her nose. The backs of her hands were red and splotchy and so was her nose after she'd blown it, but she added:

"We'll see to those tomatoes soon." She shrugged her shoulders at me and dabbed the corners of her eyes with the handkerchief.

I stood there feeling the sun hammering my skull, oblivious to the ground underfoot, and oblivious to the time passing as the years that had ticked away since Mary played for us. My eyes were filled with bright sun slanting on hard-packed clay. Then the woman said, "Yes, we'll give those tomatoes a good shot of water if it don't rain soon," and I roused myself. She was still talking and blowing her nose as I made my way out of the garden.

Back in the car the children were in each others' hair, Herman refusing to let Suzanne read his comic book and Suzanne kicking his leg with her pointed white shoe. They stared up at me with round eyes when I looked in, and retreated to the ends of the seat, studying me, frightened. I reached into my pocket for the sweets I'd been saving for later in the day. I gave them one mint each. And when they'd tucked them under their tongues, they smiled past the fright in their round brown eyes, and I divided the whole bag in half and pressed mints into their hands, dozens each, hard and sweet, I pressed them into their little hands, mints, and then I got in behind the wheel and drove away from there.

MYRON TURNER

The Crab

Late spring, the sky—a
moist, gray-blue color—gleams
like the inside of
a cracked shell.
                    A crab,
mandibles like streaks of daylight,
fills the sunlight x of the intersection.
Blue smiles of flame wink
in the half-shut, toothy joints, mud-
red and pale as flesh.
                    I stand
on the curb, like a stone
figure, askew to its eyes
in the ground, the iron
taste of earth stretched
across its smile, oblivious blue
irises peering into
the darkness.
                    On the underside
of its ferrous life, the shell buzzes
with vapours.
                    I am
smiling and frightened.

Children

No children — each
of us has had reasons —
only ourselves
and the people
we love. Now I watch
how easily you love
my daughter and my sister's
children, and shape them
to the hand and eye
of your affection.
But the beautiful, high
arc of your cheek —
a rhythm of the skies
that live in the reveries
of Cathedrals — and the skin
pulled tight over the curve
of your hip or holding
your breast like a child's
hand — milky, glowing,
a small lake where I
lie down some hour
after sunrise, and I am
weightless, and luminous —
these shapes, the colors
that delight my day-dreams
with desire, they end,
the shapes and colors
of your existence, pressed
into the understanding
of my body, and cradled
in each extinguished
breath.

ED UPWARD

the shed

i have little memory of the shed
only the creaky wooden door
and the large thick padlock
                    a veritable Fort Knox
where my uncle kept spiders
so he told me
        huge buggers
with four foot fangs
and voracious appetites
for small boys with three foot curiosities
          he would grab me
aha he would say
like Boris Karloff
      food for the spiders
i had visions of webs like fishing nets
where i hung a human fly
the hot breath of spider
emerging from the musty damp earth floor
and aging wood
     whole summers would pass
and i conspiring to unlock the mystery
like Huck Finn perfecting the plan
        but he kept close watch
and the thought of death by spider
loomed in its vampire reality

i asked questions...
how many you got in there
5 or 6
        must be crowded i thought
do spiders shit
or do they spin it out in webs
        how come
they never eat you?
they like tender little boys
why don't they break down the door?
can't stand the light
        i pictured a spider
in sunglasses

i never did learn the mystery
of that shed
and my uncle tore it down one day
claiming the spiders had all died of old age
        i never really believed him
but i saw a spider the other day
and i could have sworn it was spinning a shed

W.D. VALGARDSON

The Couch

Cramped between her husband and her father-in-law, Ruby set her jaw and stared fiercely toward town.

"The old couch is good enough," Ansford said. "It's just for sitting."

"It's got the spring through," she replied to her husband before she could stop herself. She had resolved to argue no more. They had argued since Christmas. Arguing was delaying and she was through delaying. Her mind was made up.

"You can sit to one side," Jacob countered. "You don't got to sit on the spring."

On either side, trees rose toward them in a black line, then rushed past with a jerk as though they had been attached to a string that somebody had pulled. Ruby had not been to town for twelve months and the sameness of the road depressed her. She had remembered the countryside as having more variety.

There was no traffic. They had not seen a car since they had left the island. Nor were there any houses or farms. Occasionally, a slash in the thick bush would mark the way to one of the temporary lumber camps that dotted the area. Now that the ground had thawed, most of the camps were abandoned. A few had caretakers, men who had become so bushed they could not bear going to town. When she had first been married to Ansford, Ruby had gone with him to deliver potatoes and fish to a camp. It had been a poor kind of place—a rough clearing dotted with stumps. There had been two bunkhouses on skids, piles of sawdust. There had been a caretaker, a little man with a wooden leg he had carved himself. He wore his pant leg folded back at the knee and he had painted a blue pant leg with a wide cuff, a red sock and a black shoe on the wooden stump. When they had come, he had hidden behind a sawdust pile for five minutes, coming out only when Ansford lifted a mickey of whiskey from the truck and took a drink. After three or four drinks, he had invited them into his caboose. Standing along one wall were a half dozen legs, some with green pants, some with gray, some with galoshes, others with rubber boots. The sight had given her quite a turn. She was not, Ruby had told herself then, going to become like that.

"Aren't you going awfully fast?" she asked as Ansford pulled the truck out of a skid that nearly put them into the ditch. The tie rods were worn and the truck, at the slightest excuse, was inclined to wander.

The roads were barely wide enough for two cars to pass. The edges rose toward the center to form a convex surface. No matter how much gravel was dumped during the winter, the moment the spring thaw began, the piles of stone sank from sight.

Ansford was too busy wrestling the wheel to reply. Jacob jerked his thumb at the ceiling.

"Going to rain," he said as though she could not see for herself. Clouds lay in overlapping bands like windows of gray and black stone. "We should go home." Raising his voice to be heard over the gravel drumming like hail on the underside of the truck, he repeated, "Going to rain. Better go home."

Ruby leaned forward, her face composed. She pretended she did not hear him. Ansford glanced at his father but the truck immediately swerved toward the left and he had to haul on the wheel. Although they were not long on the road, his eyes had taken on a wild look and his dark hair stuck out in spikes. He looked as if he'd had a bad fright.

"Go back," her father-in-law intoned, drawing the words out as if he were telling a ghost story. Ruby sniffed. She refused to have anything to do with him unless he had his teeth in. He had a long, lean face that was the duplicate of his son's except that it ended in a collapsed mouth that looked like a shell crater. His false teeth bulged in his shirt pocket. Despite her efforts to get him to wear them regularly, he stubbornly kept them in a sandwich bag and refused to wear them except for special occasions.

Ansford gripped the wheel so hard that the points of his knuckles were white. Before them, the road thrust into the forest like an endless knife.

Ruby secretly studied Ansford's face. Ever since she had first met her father-in-law, she had watched her husband's teeth surreptitiously, finding excuses to look in his mouth. He had already lost two teeth and that worried her. One had infected for no reason. The other had broken while he was cracking hazelnuts. Certain that this was the beginning of a dental disaster, at night, when Ansford was sound asleep, she sometimes rolled back his lip and inspected his teeth as carefully as those of a prize horse.

The three of them had started their trip at five o'clock that morning. She had been so determined to get an early start that she had gone downstairs at four to sit beside the door, her suitcase at her knee. For the trip, she wore rubber boots, slacks, two sweaters and a parka. In her suitcase she had a dress, a hat with two blue plastic daisies, black shoes and a cloth coat. She also had clothes for Ansford and Jacob.

Her husband and father-in-law had come downstairs reluctantly. Ansford came first, Jacob muttering behind him. Normally, both of them sat at the kitchen table but, for the last week, as her determination to buy a new couch had become apparent, they had taken to sitting on the old couch to show her how much wear was still in it. She had not given them an opportunity to delay her but had, on the stroke of five, the agreed-upon departure time, picked up her suitcase and started for the dock. Ansford and Jacob had trailed a couple of yards in her wake.

Neither of them was much good at hurrying at the best of times, but they had hung back like two stone anchors which she had to drag forward with every step. There were no lights in the five houses they passed. She could hear her own breathing and the swish of her boots on the grass. The lake, in this hour before dawn, was flat and dark as asphalt. She climbed down to the skiff, took her place on the middle seat, and sat stiffly, waiting, like a queen about to be transported to another country. Her suitcase pressed against her feet like a deformed child.

The wind they made as they crossed the half mile to the mainland was bitter. The ice had broken up only the week before and rafted ice still stood in piles along the shore like a line of hunchbacked dwarves. As the island faded, the mainland appeared, a solider darkness against the purple sky. Their truck was parked among a dozen vehicles owned by the people who lived on the island. There was no ferry service. Anyone who did not have a boat had to sit and flash his car lights until he was noticed. Then someone came to pick him up.

"We're going on a fool's errand," her father-in-law had said as he climbed into the truck.

When the time came, she thought, burying him would be a chore. While they were carrying the casket to the graveyard, he would still manage to mutter complaints about the inconvenience.

Dawn had been a thin red line enameled to the tops of the trees on the far shore. The line of color against the somber darkness of sky, land and water lasted only a few minutes; then thick, solid-looking clouds had filled the gap. In the gloom, lined with forest on both sides, covered over with low clouds so heavy they seemed about to fall, the road might have been the bottom of a trench.

Ruby looked up as a flurry of rain scattered over the windshield. There was a pause which was just long enough to give them hope that the rain would hold off for another hour. Thunder shook the side windows of the truck. Before the noise had faded, rain had poured down. Ahead, the road darkened. Ansford flicked on the windshield wipers. He jerked his foot off the gas pedal and let the truck glide in neutral until they had slowed to twenty.

Neither of them, she thought with a small flush of resentment as she looked at the mud, ever remembered to take off his shoes at the door. It was a constant source of aggravation. No matter how often she washed the floors, they were never clean. Both men left trails of mud wherever they went. She had tried putting a mat outside the door. When that had not worked, she had added a sign saying, "Boots here." She had spread newspaper inside the door. Finally, when it rained, she had taken to making a path of newspaper from the back door to every room in the house. The first time she had done it, they had carefully side-stepped the paper, certain it was for something special.

Ansford and she had met at an upgrading class in Winnipeg. The government was paying them both to attend so that they would not be counted as unemployed. For Ansford, squeezed between a bad fishing season and the need for new nets, it was a chance to get cash money. For Ruby, it had been a chance to get off her feet. She had been a cashier at Safeway for five years. Nine months of the year, a cold wind blew across the floor every time a customer came in or went out. The manager, thinking it would keep the customers' minds off rising grocery prices, insisted that the girls wear short skirts and shoes instead of boots. The constant standing on concrete had covered her calves with a fine mesh of red veins.

Ansford had brought her to the island late one night. Douglas McBrie had taken them across. He had said nothing to either of them but as she was climbing out of the boat, Ruby heard Ansford say, "I got her and a new outboard while I was in the city."

Ansford had told her he had a house and furniture. Her father-in-law had come as a surprise. When they arrived, the house was dark and silent. She and Ansford, tired from a long day on the road, had gone straight to bed. He had fallen asleep but she, overtired and excited by the unfamiliarity of the house that was to be her home, had been unable to sleep. Restless and not wanting to wake Ansford, she had started to go downstairs. Jacob had been standing in his nightshirt in the hallway, a tall, thin ghost with knock knees. She had been wearing a blue flannel nightgown and had her hair set with pink plastic curlers. Jacob and she had stood rooted in place. The look that crept into his face as the shock passed made her feel like the whore of Babylon. Wordlessly, she had fled, shutting the door behind her and dragging a chest of drawers against it. Ansford snored gently.

The next morning, Ansford explained to Jacob that he had married. Jacob had nodded but his eyes and the pensive set of his mouth revealed that he did not really believe it. Even the marriage certificate did not erase his lingering doubt. She and Ansford had been married twelve years, but Ruby was sure that Jacob, somewhere deep behind his eyes, believed they were living in sin.

The truck began to jerk. Ruby looked up. "What's the matter?" she asked sharply.

"Mud," Jacob yelled. His hearing was not good. To hear his own voice, he had to shout.

Ansford was pressed so close to the steering wheel that he seemed to be impaled upon it. His light brown hair looked nearly mahogany in the gloom.

Ruby braced her feet on the floor and raised herself from the seat so that she could see herself in the mirror. She had carefully set her hair the night before but already the violent motion of the truck was making it untidy. Swaying with the truck, she used her fingers to comb her hair into place. She prided herself on not letting her standards go. Many of the women did. They looked fine but the moment they got married it was as though some tightly twisted rubber band inside them was snipped and they began to fall apart. Every Friday, she religiously set her hair and changed the bed sheets. Some women she knew never combed their hair, never mind set it, and changed the linens every spring. She had told Ansford right after they married that she could not live like that.

Jacob guarded his sheets as if they were jewels. At first, she had fought with him but, gradually, she had learned to have her way without conflict. She simply waited until he left the house and, since none of the doors, including the outer ones, had locks, she went into his room, stripped and remade his bed. Occasionally, if his liver was bothering him, he still berated her, beating his fist on the table, shouting, "You leave my sheets alone, you hear! They're fine. You'll just wear them out." Of late, she had noticed that his voice was no longer sharpened by conviction.

Instructed by the country memories of parents who had moved to the city when she was only two, she had come prepared for the wrong battle. Life on the island was not endless visiting in other people's kitchens. Work seldom ceased. Leisure was idleness forced upon people by blizzards. The men cut, repaired, dug, ploughed and fished endlessly. Their wives, inundated with children, never gave over cooking, washing and mending.

Ansford geared down to second. The truck, like a cow that has tried to dodge one way, then another, and failed to escape the drover's switch, settled into a steady run. Ruby opened her purse. It was the shape and size of a shopping bag and made of purple plastic. She took out a round mirror so she could check her makeup. Her face was broad as a pumpkin. Although she constantly dieted, she was still heavy. Hard work had settled her flesh downward like buckshot in a cloth bag.

Jacob's left arm was flung along the back of the seat. He gripped the metal rail fiercely. His long legs were stretched out and his right foot jerked up and down every time the truck began to skid. His face was strained.

Ruby leaned toward him and held the mirror in front of his face. "Put in your teeth," she yelled in his ear. "You don't want to get killed looking like that."

He jerked his head around like a hawk and tried to stare down his nose at her but he could not keep his eyes off the road. He could stand in an open boat five miles from land with waves twenty feet tall flinging him about like a cork while he picked fish out of his nets, but he left the island so seldom that each journey took all his courage. Having to ride over bad roads made it worse.

"We got to go back," he shouted. "It ain't worth it to have a new couch."

Out of the corner of her eye, Ruby saw Ansford sneak a glance at her. She knew that if she showed even a moment's weakness, he would turn around and race back home.

"Keep going," she ordered. She was glad she was two years older than he. If she had not been, she would not have had the sense to know that he needed to be told what to do.

"I can't take much more of this," Ansford said. He was holding the wheel so hard that he looked as if he were going to pull it loose. He did not drive much and when he did, he preferred to travel in the center of the road at thirty miles an hour. At such times, he sat as far back on the seat as he could, his chest thrown out and his head tipped up so that he was just seeing under the sun visor.

"I got to stop," he said, his voice a defeated whine. Ahead, a driveway made a shallow loop nearly parallel with the road. A tall gas pump with a round glass top like a fish bowl sat in the center of the driveway. On the edge of the bush, a low green building squatted close to the ground. Ansford parked beside a black Chevrolet with orange ball fringe on all the windows.

They stopped at the door and, leaning in, their heads pressed together like balls, studied the interior. A naked light bulb burned over a single pool table. A group of eight Indians were frozen into position around the green felt, their eyes not looking anywhere, their ears listening to every sound. Ansford led the way to a counter with four stools.

"Bad day to be out," a fat man in tweed pants and a white shirt said. On the pocket someone had embroidered *Jimmy*. The left corner of his mouth and his left eyelid drooped. The last part of each word he said was slurred.

"Whad he say?" Jacob demanded, rifling his pockets for change.

"He said it was a bad day out," Ansford said. Ruby was sitting between them so Ansford had to lean steeply to one side to get his mouth close to his father's ear.

The Indians had started to play pool again, but when Ansford shouted, they froze into place, shining under the light like pieces of old walnut furniture.

"A bad day," Jacob repeated, nodding to himself, his eyes reflective.

He turned to Ruby, thrust his face close to hers and bellowed.

"It's a bad day for being out. We should turn around and go home."

"Coffee," Ruby said. "Black."

"Whad she say?" Jacob asked Ansford.

The Indians still had not moved.

"Coffee," Ansford replied at the top of his voice.

Jacob nodded vigorously. "Me, too."

Jimmy brought their order for them, dropping the heavy white crockery with a clatter.

"You must be Jimmy," Ruby said.

The fat man shook his head. "I'm Bill."

"Whad he say?" Jacob asked.

"My name's Bill," the fat man shouted.

They all studied his pocket. He looked down.

"Got these shirts at an auction," he explained, raising his voice as if he were talking to a multitude. "They all got different names on them."

"It says Jimmy," Jacob insisted.

Before Bill could explain again, Ruby said, "I don't remember you from last year."

"Christmas," he replied. "Under new ownership. Had a sign. Wind blew it down." He shouted each phrase so that Jacob could hear.

"You from the city?" Ruby asked. He nodded. "I seen your white shirt and I knew." She shot a glance full of reproval at Ansford. "My husband's got a white shirt but he won't wear it but once a year."

Ansford leaned closer to his coffee. He had spread his elbows on the counter and was counting the different kinds of candy bars. There were five kinds he had not eaten.

"I'd give a dollar to go back home right now," Jacob declared.

"You'd think we made him come." Ruby pressed her lips together in mild indignation the way she might with a child. "He complains all the time but if we leave him alone for half an hour, he comes looking for us."

"The road's bad further on," Bill said.

"You seen these?" Jacob asked. He dug into his jacket pocket and held out a rooster carved from a forked stick. "I sold lots of these. Dollar apiece."

Bill saw Ruby looking at the name on his pocket. "Tomorrow, I'll be Norman. The day after that Robert."

"If you bought five for a dollar," Jacob said, peering at Bill's face, trying to see if there was a flicker of interest, "you could sell them for a dollar seventy-five."

"How do you know who you are?" Ansford burst out. "Every day you've got a different name."

"Who," Bill said, turning to look square into his face, "ever knows who he is?"

Jacob was holding the rooster between his thumb and forefinger, twirling it around so that all its good points would be revealed. Bill turned back and nearly got the rooster in the eye.

"He likes to whittle," Ruby said. "Finish up," she said to Ansford. Ansford was trying to make his coffee last as long as possible.

Bill reached a large hand under the counter and drew out a brown envelope. "Would you deliver this to the garage? It's a check for some car parts. They won't send any more until they get paid."

Ruby slid off the stool. "Not much business here." She took the envelope, and squashed it into her jacket pocket.

"Suits me." He folded his hands over his stomach. "Had a stroke. Can't do more than a little."

"I wish you luck." She said it with solemnity the way she might to someone who had declared he was going to jump off a cliff and try to fly.

"I got a pension."

Ruby adjusted her head scarf and started for the door. Behind her, Bill called, "It ain't much but everybody's got to have something to keep him going."

They hurried through the rain that cut across the sky. The drops fell with such force that the water might have collected around a center of lead. Inside the cab, Jacob said petulantly, "If you'd a just waited, I'd a sold him some carving." When he felt unjustly treated he had a way of drawing his eyebrows together until they nearly touched.

The road was as slick as if it had been greased. Rain fell steadily. The ditches were full. Ruts had become long bands of nearly black water.

Jacob sat deep in thought for the first mile and she thought he was sulking, but all at once he straightened up, looked at them both and said, "He must be hard of hearing. He certainly shouts a lot."

They traveled the next thirty miles in silence. Because of the rain, there was nothing to see and Ruby and Jacob fell into a light doze until Ansford startled them by sharply calling out a warning.

They were approaching a bog. The land on either side of the road was a sea of moss. Full-grown trees were no more than three feet high. When they crossed the edge of the bog, it was as if the truck had been grabbed from behind. Their bodies were flung forward. Ansford gunned the motor, accelerating as fast as he could. The truck jerked so violently that it felt as if the transmission had been ripped out. Ansford slammed the truck into second, then first. It was no use. The truck slowed; the motor coughed and died. Ruby could feel the wheels sinking.

They sat, staring into the rain as if hypnotized. There was nothing before them except empty road and endless forest. On either side of them there was forest. Behind them, blurred by rain, the trees went on until the road disappeared and the two dark lines converged.

"We can't stay here," she said.

"We're twenty miles from town," Ansford protested.

"We can't go back. We've come too far."

Ansford looked out the rear window. When he turned back, the skin on his face was tight as though someone was pulling it from behind.

"We should of stayed home," Jacob wailed. "I told you. Every year it's the same. The ice goes off the lake and she's got to go to town for something."

"Let's go," she said, her voice determined. "Sitting here talking isn't going to get us anywhere."

She gave Ansford a shove with her hip.

"I'm not going," Jacob screamed. "I'm an old man. My legs won't take it."

Ruby gave Ansford another shove. He opened his door and got out. He lifted Ruby's suitcase out of the wooden box on the back of the truck. As they started away, Jacob yelled, once more, "I'm not going. I don't have to go just because you say so."

The rain beat on them as they ploughed through the mud. Mud clung to their boots like paste. Mud splashed up their legs. With every step, Ruby had to pull her foot loose. The ground was a quagmire. Each time she lifted her feet, more mud clung to them. After fifteen minutes her feet were so grotesquely large that she had to stop. Behind her, she heard water splash. She turned around. Jacob was standing nearly on her heels. His shoulders were hunched together. Water streamed through his thin hair and poured in a steady stream from his nose. Bending over to protect it from the rain, she reached into her purse and took out a second rain cap of clear plastic. She pulled the cap over Jacob's head and tied the bow beneath his chin.

Seeing his dismay, she shouted, "Nobody's going to see you."

Ansford came up to them with sticks of willow which he had cut. He had flattened one end. With these, they pried the mud from their boots.

The rain swept down, engulfing them, breaking over their heads and shoulders like surf.

Ruby tried various strategies. She tried to pick her way carefully, placing her feet where the gravel was thickest. All that happened was that both mud and gravel came up together. She tried walking on the high spots on the theory that the ground would not be so wet. Then, in the hope that the water would wash her boots clean, she walked in the ruts. Nothing worked. After a while, the weight of mud on each foot was so great that she had to swing her legs stiffly from the hips.

When they reached what she had estimated was the second mile, she checked her watch. It was fifteen after twelve and they had eighteen miles to go. She looked back. The truck had disappeared behind a curtain of rain. In front of them was an endless stretch of mud and sodden trees. All she wanted was to reach the town. The thought that they still had eighteen miles to go made her waver. At the moment, if she could have, she might have agreed to return home. Since that was impossible, she forced herself ahead by thinking about lying in the bed at the hotel and watching TV.

At one-thirty they had to stop to rest. They had walked the last half mile on rising ground and the going had been easier. Now, the ground sloped down again. As she stood, looking along the road, Ruby's thigh muscles felt as if they had been pulled loose. Her knees felt as if the joints had been ground down with pumice. Water was seeping through the seams of her jacket.

"We've got to keep going," Ansford said. Shorter and broader than his father, he still looked lean and hard. He was slightly bandy-legged, and his wet trousers clinging to him emphasized the two outward curves. Water dripped from his plaid cap. He took it off and wrung it out.

He was slow to make up his mind, but once he had there was no stopping him.

They started off again. Lifting her feet hurt so much that Ruby thought of taking off her boots and socks. Less mud, she was sure, would cling to her skin. She rejected the idea because the mud, only recently thawed, was still cold. Her breathing was beginning to be labored, her breath whistling in her head. She shivered and wished that she had something hot to drink.

Darkness settled over them so gradually that she was not aware of the fading light until she began to find it difficult to see Ansford. Earlier, she had been worried about being caught on the road in the dark. Now, she was too tired to care.

The rain still fell, no longer in torrents, but in a steady, chilling drizzle. Her legs were soaked. Her face was numb.

The walking had turned to stumbling. There were pauses between steps. At last, they stopped and huddled together.

"How far do you think it is?" she asked.

"Ten miles," Ansford replied, "maybe eleven."

"We've walked all day," Jacob cried, his voice thin as a spider web.

They staggered forward for another hour. Ruby's feet, heavy as cast iron, dragged through the mud. When she realized that Jacob no longer was behind her, she called Ansford. They started back. They found Jacob sitting in a rut, struggling feebly to get up. Ansford took one arm, Ruby the other. Between them, they heaved him to his feet. Since he could go no farther, they led him to the edge of the forest. Even here, under a canopy of branches, rain sifted down upon them. They stood dumbly, unable to see, too tired to want to do anything except lie down and rest.

They turned Jacob in a half-circle, positioned him between two saplings rising from a single root. They pushed him down, cramming him between the two trunks so that he was firmly held in place. Ruby sat on the left, Ansford on the right. Oblivious of the rain or their aching bodies, they fell asleep.

Ruby woke up cold. She could not feel anything from the waist down and, at first, she was not sure where she was. Her legs were stretched out before her like two dead weights pinning her to the sodden ground. She lifted her left arm to pluck at her parka and tried to pull it more tightly about her. The clouds might have been molded from clay. She was, she realized, still leaning against Jacob. His chin rested on his chest. She knew he was still alive because she could see his nose dilate with each breath. Ansford had fallen over and lay on his back, his mouth open. She wondered, her thoughts distant, detached, how it was that he had not drowned. Mercifully, the rain was only a fine mist.

Grasping the tree with one hand, she pulled herself to her knees. Gradually, as she kneaded her legs, the blood came back into them. She dragged herself to her feet. She did not dare let go of the tree. Her suitcase, she noticed, lay beside Ansford's hand. She was glad that she had wrapped all their belongings in plastic.

She reached out with her toe and jabbed Ansford. He did not move. She kicked harder, digging her toe into his ribs. He opened his eyes, lay staring at the clouds, then closed his eyes again. She kicked him hard enough to hurt her big toe.

"Get up," she said. Her throat was so cold that the words were a croak. "You've got to get up." She had never quit shivering and every time she shut her eyes she had the sensation of falling. She knew that she could do nothing without him.

He opened his eyes, coughed twice, rolled over and pushed himself up. He looked as if he had been dug out of a grave. He was covered from head to foot in mud. Pressed into the mud were twigs, leaves, grass, pine needles, even a couple of feathers. His hair was matted, his eyes sunken.

"Jacob," Ruby said. She slapped him on the back. There was a wet smack. He groaned. She hit him twice more. He stared dumbly, his eyes unfocused. They each took an arm and because they were weak with hunger and cold had to strain to pull him free. At first, he was a dead weight. They walked him in a tight circle, around and around in the wet grass. His legs kept collapsing. One moment, his legs held him, then they gave out and he dropped to his knees. Each time, grunting, one hand under each armpit, the other braced just above his elbow, they levered him up. It was like walking a horse with severe colic.

"We'd better get going," Ansford said. He picked up the suitcase.

The day before, mud had clung to their boots. Now, the mud was so wet that it was the consistency of tomato soup. With each step, Ruby sank past her ankles. She could think of nothing except being dry and warm and eating platters of food. Gradually, walking warmed her, but her hunger grew into a savage pain. Even that, however, passed into a dull ache. She felt as though she had swallowed a large, smooth stone.

It was noon when they heard a noise like distant thunder. At first, they ignored it. They staggered forward, their bodies lurching from side to side.

Lifting her eyes from the mud, Ruby looked past the rounded hump of Ansford's back. Moving slowly toward them was a tractor. Ansford looked up and stopped. She saw his shoulders settle as though air had been holding them up and had suddenly been released. She thought he might fall down but, instead, he stood wedged in the mud like a fence post. Ruby stopped, grateful not to have to lift her feet again. She felt that if someone touched her with the tip of his finger she would topple to the ground and be unable to rise. She could hear Jacob splashing behind her. When he came abreast, she caught his arm sharply.

He had been walking automatically, his body moving independently of any thought. Her fingers on his jacket sleeve stopped him as completely as if someone had turned off a switch. He stood and trembled, docile as a tamed animal. The tractor churned toward them.

The tractor driver's back was covered in mud kicked up by the chains. He grinned at them, then got down and gave each of them a hand up.

"Bill at halfway house phoned to say you were bringing some money he owed me. When you didn't arrive, I figured I'd better come looking for you."

"Spent the night in the bush," Ansford replied.

"Looks like it," the driver said and turned the tractor around.

There was no place to sit so they rode standing, Ruby and Jacob on either side of the driver, Ansford on the hitch. They climbed down in the middle of Main Street. The rain had melted the mud just enough to spread it evenly over them. Jacob still had on Ruby's head cover.

The tractor driver promised to bring in the truck; then Ruby led the way to the hotel. They rented a room with a double bed and had a cot put in for Jacob.

Ruby had a hot shower with her clothes on. When the water running along the bottom of the tub was no longer gray, she peeled off her parka, waited for the water to clear again, then undressed completely. She washed, changed into the clothes she had brought, then helped Jacob into the bathroom. He moved stiffly. He tried to undo his jacket and could not, so she stood him in the tub and turned on the shower. She undid his parka. The warm water started to revive him. She helped him off with his sweater, undid his shirt and pulled it off. She threw everything into the tub to be washed later. He let her pull off his socks but when she started to undo his pants, he protested. She told him to be quiet or she'd call Ansford to come and hold him still.

When he stood in nothing but his long underwear, she gave him the soap and left.

Ansford lay curled before the door on a wad of old newspapers which the desk clerk had given them. All the time he waited, he shivered and jerked. Except for his eyes, he was completely caked in mud and, as it dried, it stiffened so that he looked like an unfinished statue.

Ruby laid out their clothes. She did not have much room in the suitcase but she managed to bring a change of clothes for each of them, including a white shirt for both men.

While Ansford was washing, she took their dirty clothes to the basement of the hotel and washed and dried them. When she went back upstairs, Ansford and Jacob looked scrubbed and brushed. The three of them went to the dining room and ate two platters of ham and eggs each and drank twelve cups of coffee between them. By the time they were finished, they all had a satisfied, glazed look.

Ruby led them down the sidewalk to the Red and White Hardware and Furniture store. A salesman in a brown suit scurried out from behind a small forest of pole lamps. Ruby scanned the room. The salesman, his eyes full of anticipation, his hands washing themselves in little circular motions, darted this way and that.

"I heard you've got a blue couch for sale," Ruby said. "We need a new one."

The salesman lifted himself up on his toes as though he was a ballet dancer and, wobbling, looked across the array of couches. "I've got a nice red one," he said.

"You've got a blue one," Ruby insisted. "With pansies. I heard at Christmas you had it."

"I sold that months ago," he said.

"I wanted blue," Ruby insisted.

The salesman asked her to wait, hurried away and came back in a minute with a catalogue. He pointed out a picture of a blue chesterfield and offered to order it.

"It's not the way I imagined it." Ruby pursed her lips in disapproval.

"I got others,'" the salesman said.

"No," Ruby answered. "It isn't what I thought." Her decision made, she turned around and herded the two men before her.

"I told you," Jacob whispered indignantly to Ansford. He moved his teeth about with his tongue. "I told you she wouldn't buy it. Every year it's the same." His voice carried all the way to the other side of the street.

Ruby ignored her father-in-law and stood, her hands on her hips, looking with satisfaction up and down Center Street. It was only a block long but the stores were deep and contained a host of objects. There were women in town whom she knew well enough to visit and on Sunday there was a service at the church.

The rain had stopped. The clouds were breaking up to reveal a clear, bright sky. The street, covered with a thin layer of water, looked as if it had been plated with silver. The signs of the stores, swept clean by rain, were bright and shiny.

"All that," Jacob complained, "for nothing." But there was no force in his voice, for he was squinting, trying to read a sign on the movie house a half block away. In any case, Ansford was paying him no attention. He had turned halfway around to try to identify the half dozen men who were sitting in the window of the garage.

"What can't be helped shouldn't be mourned," Ruby said, seeing her reflection in a puddle as shiny as a newly minted silver dollar. She tilted her hat so that the flowers showed to more advantage. "We can't," she added, "go anywhere until the road dries. There's today and tomorrow. We'll just have to make the best of it."

MIRIAM WADDINGTON

Ukrainian Church

Little father your
rhythmic black robe
against white snow
improvises you
a black note
on a white keyboard;

let me follow
into your churchbarn
through the gate
to the onion domes
where your carrot
harvest burns
a fire of candles,

let me follow
in the cool light
as you move through
God's storehouse
as you put the bins
in order as you set
each grain in place;

let me follow
as your voice
moves in the
familiar liturgy
through the low caves
of Gregorian chant
and let me hear
little father

how you pray
for all your geese
for the cow fertile
at Easter and the
foundations of new
houses to be strong
and firmly set;

let me hear
how you beseech
for all your people
a clear road, an
open gate and
a new snowfall
fresh, dazzling,
white as birchbark.

Fortunes

There is something in all of us
pure and unconsumable;
after the forest fires
on the logged-over hillsides
you find the stubborn flowering
of fireweed or a green tree
hung with a grab-bag of prophecies:
you will live long you will go on ocean voyages
you will be lucky in love or unlucky
beware the queen of spades a handsome stranger
will come into your life the choices
are dazzling.

But whatever you do
it will end the same;
we are not all lucky and the stranger came
but stayed a stranger   we lived
unhappily ever after and the queen of spades
dug my grave; after the ten thousandth evening
of dumb show and furious pantomime
fed up with Punch and Judy
I went out into the autumn night
to cry my anger to the stone-blind fields
just as I was, untraditional, North American,
Jewish, Russian, and rootless in all four,
religious, unaffiliated, and held
in a larger-than-life seize of hate.

It was then I felt my own purity:
I felt the young girl in me
still like a green tree growing,
tall and rooted, with a promise of flowering,
whatever bastardy flower I could flower with now,
a *shloime-kapoir* Solomon-upside-down flower;
and why not? I always think of the Russian word
for soul, *dusha*, and the dusty Slavic village
smelling so sweet with the grass uncut
and the white lilacs blooming, like a homecoming
for my homeless half-and-half soul.

And I felt a kind of raised eyebrow
yes-this-is-me   this is no one else,
not the laidly worm of Spindlestone,
no longer the bewitched princess
but a wonderful living statue of marble stone
with her garments sculptured,
sailing against the wind of death.

From a Dead Poet's Book

There was the sound
of your breathing,
and your voice
saying *forever*,
a word from a line
in a dead poet's book.

There was light
from a candle
there was a wall
and a forest and
darkness an island
with yourself

And myself floating
from sleep we
watched last autumn's
love apples fanning
and tossing on seas
in the darkness,

And through darkness
and light felt
snow on the rooftops
in a distant city in
a lonely nightwatch;
there was the sound

Of your breathing,
like a burning garland
forever hung above us,
winter burned   apples
glittered and words
froze on the branches;

And everywhere in
darkness was *forever*
and everywhere in
darkness was your
voice and everywhere
the distant city and
everywhere (I almost
said) everywhere was
my love.

The Nineteen Thirties Are Over

The nineteen thirties
are over; we survived
the depression, the Sacco-
Vanzetti of childhood
saw Tom Mooney smiling
at us from photographs,
put a rose on the grave
of Eugene Debs, listened
to our father's stories
of the Winnipeg strike and
joined the study groups
of the OBU always keeping
one eye on the revolution.

Later we played records
with thorn needles, Josh
White's *Talking Union* and
Prokofief's *Lieutenant Kije*,
shuddered at the sound of
bells and all those wolves
whirling past us in snow

on the corner of Portage
and Main, but in my mind
summer never ended on the
shores of Gimli where we
looked across to an Icelandic
paradise we could never see
the other side of; and I
dreamed of Mexico and shining
birds who beckoned to me
from the gold-braided lianas
of my own wonder.

These days I step out
from the frame of my wind-
battered house into Toronto
city; somewhere I still
celebrate sunlight, touch
the rose on the grave of
Eugene Debs but I walk
carefully in this land
of sooty snow; I pass the
rich houses and double
garages and I am not really
this middle-aged professor
but someone from
Winnipeg whose bones ache
with the broken revolutions
of Europe, and even now
I am standing on the heaving
ploughed-up field
of my father's old war.

eography

Mia... he big yellow
pantsuit where the ocean
is louder than the sighs
of old age; Chicago is
a huge hot gun sending
smoke into the sky for
1000 miles to Winnipeg;
New York is a bright sharp
hypodermic needle and the
Metropolitan Opera singing
Wagner on winter afternoons,
and my own Toronto is an
Eaton's charge account adding
to the music in a Henry Moore
skating rink; Montreal was
once an Iroquois city huddled
around a mountain under a cross
and now is the autoroute to
an Olympic dream; everything
has changed, all the cities
are different, but Manitoba
oh Manitoba, you are still
a beautiful green grain
elevator storing the sunlight
and growing out of the black
summer earth.

Provincial

My childhood
was full of people
with Russian accents
who came from
Humble Saskatchewan
or who lived in Regina
and sometimes
visited Winnipeg
to bring regards
from their frozen
snowqueen city.

In those days
all the streetcars
in the world slept
in the Elmwood
car-barns and the
Indian moundbuilders
were still wigwammed
across the river
with the birds
who sang in the bushes
of St. Vital.

Since then I have
visited Paris
Moscow London
and Mexico City
I saw golden roofs
onion domes and the
most marvellous
canals, I saw people
sunning themselves
in Luxembourg Gardens
and on a London parkbench
I sat beside a man
who wore navy blue socks
and navy blue shoes
to match.

All kinds of miracles:
but I would not trade
any of them for the
empty spaces, the
snowblurred geography
of my childhood.

The New Seasons: Light and Dark

1

In winter
we tread dead names
in all our cities,
mornings
we imagine origins
and read
our country's history
in our own pulse
and vein.

In spring
we find ourselves
in blades of grass
in fields in provinces,
and listening
we hear
old prairie winds
composing the refrain
of secret legacies.

2
In autumn
we stand on banks
of asphalt
as the night descends
and wonder
will this city space
survive
to hear our rivers sing
of daylight and clean water
above the roar of words
and flooding numbers
that issue from machines?

3
It may be
citizens will endure
to march like Birnam Wood
against the whim
of buttons the mindless
push of levers and
the vanities that seethe
in board-rooms;

Then citizens
will calculate with ploughs
the contours of each corner
of this earth,
and they will plant
their wheat and flowers
and raise
the flag of life
to celebrate our love
of country
and declare ourselves
rooted and revealed
in place.

ARMIN WIEBE

These Troubled Times

Did you ever have a day when you couldn't get nothing done because it seemed like nobody wanted to mind their own business? Just one bother after another? Well today it seems like it is such a day. Me and my boy, Doft, he's twelve, are trying to get the manure shovelled out of the pig barn and so far we haven't filled up the manure sled even once. First Oata comes to get the car keys from me so she can go to the store, which shouldn't take very long, but she has to tell me first what all she heard on the radio before she came to the barn and one of the things is that there will be a Progressive Conservative meeting at the Gutenthal curling rink next week Tuesday. Oata has just hardly driven off the yard when little Frieda, who is seven, comes from the house and says somebody is phoning for me. So I go to the house and it's some lawyer outfit that wants to take away a farm from a guy called Siemens because there is a receivership on it. So I tell him that my land doesn't even have a rowboat leave alone a receivership. He swears on the phone and says, "Am I speaking to Jack Siemens?" "For sure not," I say. "I'm Yasch, not Jack." And he wants to know how he can get a hold of Jack Siemens. So I tell him about the six Jack Siemenses I know and that if he is mixed up with Jake Siemens there are about seven more at least and four yet that write themselves 'Jac.' But I don't think any of them have ships on their land, but old J.J.P. Siemens in Prachadarp was born on a ship coming from Russia so he was a Canadian before the rest of the family. And I tell that lawyer that I'll send him a bill for the information.

When I get back outside Hingst Heinrichs stops in the yard with his Ford truck that has custom cab, CB and mag wheels. When he climbs out I see that he is wearing one of those Farmers Revivalist caps like you can see on TV. I didn't know that the caps were brown and white because me and Oata still watch that old 11-inch black and white that I got cheap from Ha Ha Nickel when he had to buy himself a color set. Some people around here now have booster cable TV and Ha Ha Nickel's son-in-law Pug Peters has one of those dishwasher TV things in his yard that they say can get 200 stations.

Anyway, Hingst tells me that there will be a meeting by the Elks Hall in town next week and that every farmer that doesn't want the family farm to disappear should go to that meeting. I look at him and wonder what he means by a family farm when he has three sections all himself and it says 'The Hingst Heinrichs Corporation' on his truck. But I just say, "I figure my family farm is okay!" Hingst looks at me. "Yeah, I guess you would say that." I know he is thinking yeah sure, Yasch, you married yourself a farm so it didn't cost you nothing. I know he is thinking that and it's true. I married myself with fat Oata Needarp after her father Nobah Naze died and I am farming a half-section all paid for and even some money in the bank. And Hingst says that even if I figure I'm okay I should come anyway because it looks like maybe the bank is going to try to close Pug Peters's farm and at the meeting farmers are going to decide if they can stop the bank. "In tough times," he says, "we have to stick together." I smile a bit and say what Shaftich Shreeda said when he ran for the NDP: "When the going gets tough, the tough get going." And I say that if I get my manure shovelled out of the pig barn I'll come to the meeting. Hingst laughs. "Yasch, you cheap bugger. Why don't you build a decent pig barn with an automatic barn cleaner?" I just look at him and say, "Like I said, my family farm is okay."

Hingst Heinrichs isn't away five minutes when Yut Yut Leeven's boys, Laups and Lowtz, drive in the yard. I say to Doft, "It's a good thing I'm a Flat German all full with *Wehrlosigkeit* otherwise I would stick these guys with the pitchfork already," because Laups and

Lowtz can spread the bullshit as good as a Better Bilt Honey Wagon. But Laups's wife is pretty good friends with Oata and I mean I used to spread a bit of manure with these guys too, in the Neche beer parlor where we would see all kinds of Flat Germans drinking beer that didn't want to be seen in the parlor at home. Yut Yut Leeven used to be the biggest farmer in Gutenthal and Laups and Lowtz would never let you forget it. I used to be scared of them when I was small because they were so rich and I was just a poor boy weeding beets by their place. But after I had weeded beets there for three weeks I wasn't scared no more. I guess you could say we are friends. The Leevens aren't the biggest farmers no more, like the brothers only have a section and a half between them. Sure, they got their farm from their Futtachi, so it didn't cost them so much, but I don't know if it was something that Yut Yut told them when he was living his last days in hospital or if the Leeven boys are smarter than everybody else. Maybe it's because they were well off when they were young so it didn't seem so important when they were older. But that time when we went to Laups's cabin by Mouse Lake, me and him went fishing early in the morning. We didn't catch anything but we had a long talk in the boat and Laups said to me, "You know Yasch, in this world a man has to decide how much he needs to live on, and then be satisfied with that. How much farm does one man need?" And I was thinking to myself, yeah sure, it's easy to say that when you have all you need already, because I had an application in to borrow myself money to buy Pracha Platt's half-section. But the Credit Committee from the Credit Union said no. They said I didn't have enough farming experience and not enough equipment for so much land. The next week I found out that Ha Ha Nickel had bought Pracha Platt's farm for his son-in-law, Pug Peters. Well for sure, I was pretty mad about that for a while, because I was once quite a bit crazy about Ha Ha Nickel's skinny daughter Sadie, but she let Pug Peters get into her first and now he got the land that I wanted.

But Pug he hailed out that year and I had a good crop even if I could hardly get the thrashing finished because that old 27 John Deere combine just didn't want to work any more. Still the price of wheat was good so I bought myself a newer Massey for almost all cash and I didn't have to go in the hole to keep farming. I was farming 100 pigs, too, not in a fancy barn with a manure pit and all kinds of fans, just the ordinary old barn. Sure it's hard work but at least a person can make a bit of money and so what if some of the neighbors complained that my pigs were stinking up all of Gutenthal. I know what money smells like. I put the manure on the fields, too, so I didn't have to buy myself fertilizer with borrowed money and the next year when that old Fordson Major tractor needed an overhaul I bought myself a 4010 John Deere that Puch Panna had traded off on a Versatile four-wheel drive. I got a good deal because no farmer wants such a small outfit no more.

Still I wanted to be a bigshot farmer and when Fuchtich Froese got sick and had to sell his three quarters I tried to buy, at least one quarter, but the Bank of Commerce manager wouldn't give me a loan except if I got somebody to co-sign for me. So I just went and got a case of beer instead. That was the year before little Doft would have to go to school so me and Oata were talking about it all and we had never gone for a trip when we got married so at Christmas time I shipped all the pigs and we slaughtered the chickens and I borrowed the cows to Zoop Zack Friesen for a month and we went to Florida.

Sure, Yasch Siemens isn't a bigshot farmer like the others, but it's not so bad really. With only a half-section I can really farm it, and I don't think I have any more wild oats and mustard than the neighbors who use all that Avadex BW and Hoe-grass stuff they show sliding on a curling rink on TV. In the winter time I read things about organic farming and I don't know but for a small outfit like mine it seems to work. A farmer always has worries but it sure doesn't seem so bad when you don't have to worry about feeding the bank manager's family, the lawyer's family and the implement dealer's family. But then Oata helps, too. She makes a big garden and we have our own chickens, pigs, cows and things so we hardly even have to worry about feeding the storeman's family yet, too. Doft sometimes wants to know how come he can't have one of those games that you play with the TV like the neighbors' boys have but I just laugh and say that while those guys are playing with themselves on TV he can play with their girlfriends.

Anyway, I'm running out of the furrow here with this story. Laups and Lowtz Leeven come by the yard and they are both laughing like crazy when they climb out of the cab.

"Hey Yasch, did you get your mail today?"

"No, Oata is getting it."

"Look what we got."

"Yeah, look." Lowtz holds out a small card. I take it from him. It is a membership card for the Gutenthal Progressive Conservative Party and it has Lowtz's name written on it and is signed by Haustig Neefeld who is president for the Gutenthal PCs.

"I got one too," Laups says and shows me his.

"Two timers," I say. "Bunch of two-timing Liberals."

"Now now Yasch. Don't be so fromm. I'll bet Oata will bring you one from the mail, too. It seems like everyone in Gutenthal got one, even Shaftich Shreeda!"

"So who is paying for all this? That macaroni baloney fella?"

"Maybe it's Clark's pork 'n beans," Lowtz says.

"Nobody knows for sure, except that Puch Panna said that Haustig Neefeld said that last week he got all these membership forms in the mail with money to pay for the cards. So Yasch, I bet Oata will bring you home a Conservative card."

"Well, Yasch, it won't be so bad. I mean you already have a blue Sunday suit."

Sure enough, Oata drives in the yard and right away holds up the PC card with my name on it. "Yasch, Yasch, what is loose with you? Did you give money to these penzels without asking me?"

"No, no Oata. You think I would throw money away? Everybody in Gutenthal got one in the mail, even drains like these guys here."

"Oh, and here I thought maybe some screws were getting loose in your head. Do they have lunch by these PC meetings?"

"Oh sure," says Lowtz. "Haustig Neefeld's mumchi and Fuchtich Froese's daughters have been making lunch already for a whole week."

"Good, then we can go to the meeting. If you can eat free, why not?"

"That's the stuff, Oata. We'll see you at the PC meeting."

The Leeven boys drive away and Oata goes in the house. I stand there looking at the PC membership card, trying to figure out why they would want to have me for a member, especially when I have always voted for the NDP. And the reason I vote for the NDP is because when I was thirteen I was heista kopp in love with Shaftich Shreeda's daughter Fleeda. And Shaftich Shreeda was the only person in Gutenthal who had the nerves to vote for the NDP and tell other people about it. He was voting for the NDP when most of the Flat Germans still voted for the Social Credit and the NDP had only changed from the CCF a little while. Sure, there were lots of jokes about the Canadian Common Fools and the Cooperative Cow Fornicators and then when it changed to NDP they said No Damn Policy. But then it seemed like the Gutenthallers got tired with Social Credit. It seemed like it could only work if you had lots of oil wells and those that talked the loudest about More Debt or Social Credit moved themselves away to BC. So in Gutenthal people voted PC again because they figured it had been so good with Honest John Diefenbaker. I vote NDP because with Shaftich Shreeda's daughter Fleeda was the first time in my life that I was heista kopp in love and even after Fleeda went off to be a missionary and married herself with somebody in Africa and it's all water through the culvert now, it warms me up a little bit to vote for the NDP. My wife Oata never tells me who she votes for. She says it's nobody's business, it's like why you have a door on the beckhouse.

It's been pretty good being married with Oata, what is it now, twelve years. That's how old my boy, Doft, is and Frieda is seven. The ball team laughered themselves good when we got married a little bit in a hurry. I mean, we didn't even wait for the preacher to have time, we just went to the judge in Emerson and got married there. I think it was just as good as in the Gutenthal church. At least we didn't have to feed everybody buns and baloney in the church cellar after the wedding. Yeah, they laughed when I married myself with fat Oata Needarp and the guys on the ball team were marrying themselves with all kinds of thin women. But now their wives are all pretty fat and my Oata is still slowly getting thinner. It happened while she was in the hospital with little Doft and she was reading in this States magazine about a woman that was even fatter than Oata and how she got quite thin. Oata sneaked that magazine home from the hospital and she didn't even tell me nothing about it. She started doing the stuff that was in the magazine and very slowly she started to get thinner. I mean it was going so slowly that I didn't even notice it really, you know how it is when you live with a person every day for years, you forget to look real close, until that time when Doft was six years old and Frieda was one, Laups Leeven and his wife, Tusch, invited us to come for the weekend to Mouse Lake and before we went there Oata drove to town and when she came back she called me upstairs into the bedroom. She was dressed up in a bathing suit and it was like I had never seen Oata before and I said to her that we would have to leave the lights on at night some time. Oata poked me where my belly was hanging over my belt and said, "You think I want to look at that?" Sure, Oata isn't skinny like Sadie Nickel, who after three kids is still thin like she was fifteen, but if they ever have a Mrs. Gutenthal contest I will sure enter my Oata.

I guess you could say that I'm one of the still ones in the land. After I got married with Oata I stopped to pitch for the ball team. I don't know, but it seemed like one part of my life was finished, that the ball team was something I didn't need no more. I haven't even gone to look at the ball games but now Doft is twelve and he has been asking if he can go so maybe I will start again. I've been teaching Doft how to be a pitcher and he likes it, but it seems that now when the kids go to school in town they don't get the same chance to play baseball like I did in the Gutenthal school. I'm a still one in church, too. Sure, me and Oata go to church every Sunday like most others here. It's a good place to rest after a week's hard work. But after I gave that testimony one time nobody has asked me to do anything more.

I hardly even go to the curling rink in winter. When they first built it I curled two winters but when a man gets older it just seems like dummheit to stand on the ice when it's thirty below and freeze your feet. Besides, now that they have artificial ice in town they didn't even make ice in Gutenthal last winter and those only that are all stone in the head would want to curl from before thrashing is finished till seeding time like they do now. No, I'm not one of those that is always away at meetings for this and that. I vote when there is a vote and that's it.

Still, now that I have a Conservative card it bothers me. There it is on a piece of paper, my name, connected up with politics. Sure it must be a joke, but when your name is on a piece of paper it can lead to all kinds of things. I just feel like something will happen. I try to shove it out of my head and think only about getting the barn clean. Doft has been doing most of the shovelling while my head has been driving all over the place. I am proud about my boy Doft. He is strong and does good in school. When he was being born I was sitting in the waiting room in the hospital sweating because it was taking Oata so long and I was alone there. It was the middle of the night and I was worrying about Oata and about me, wondering if I was strong enough to be a father. And I was thinking about what kind of a person I was and I could only see all the bad things about myself, how lazy I was, and all the times I went to drink beer with the ball team, or that time on Halloween when lots of flax straw bales were burned. Or that time me and Hova Jake picked up Susch and Tusch from Sommerfeld and said we are going to hear Barry Moore in Dominion City but instead went driving around and did lots of things that Barry Moore probably preached against. Yeah, I gribbled about all this till my shirt was as wet as it gets at haying time but in the end the head straightens it all out and the nurse came to tell me to come look at my boy.

In Saturday's mail comes an announcement about the PC meeting. It says that the guest speaker will be Yeeat Shpanst. That's all it says. Yeeat Shpanst. It doesn't say who Yeeat Shpanst is or where he is from or what he will talk about. Well, I figure maybe the real PCers know who he is, I mean nobody knew who Joe Clark was neither. And I think to myself that maybe it would be nice to have a good Flat German in the government, except that it always seems like the Flat Germans that get in the government always pretty soon forget that they are Flat Germans and when you see them on the CBC news they sound just like a radio, not like maybe they weeded beets or shovelled manure when they were young.

Anyway on Sunday we are driving to church with the kids and all of a sudden Doft says, "Hey, Papuh, look at that there on the hydro pole." I look and stop the car. There stapled on the pole just like you always have when there is a vote is a poster that says YEEAT SHPANST—TOMORROW'S LEADERSHIP TODAY. I look down the road and see that every other pole has a Yeeat Shpanst sign.

"Huy Yuy Yuy," Oata says. "Maybe we should rip some off to take home for starting the fire in the stove." She pokes me in the ribs with her elbow. Those signs are every place. On the side of Pracha Platt's old barn there are a bunch of signs stapled to make the letters YS.

Walking the church in it seems like everybody is fuscheling about Yeeat Shpanst. I take a bulletin from Forscha Friesen who has never figured out anything else to do with himself after all these years and sit down. Even in the bulletin under announcements it tells about Yeeat Shpanst's meeting at the Gutenthal curling rink.

Well for sure on Tuesday evening the Gutenthal curling rink is full with people. So full that they have to move the meeting out from the waiting room to the ice part. It's a good thing somebody thought about bringing a loudspeaker system because usually at the curling rink you don't need one for a meeting. At least not if only the Gutenthallers come but it seems like every Flat German between here and Yanzeed has come to Gutenthal. And lots of English and French too it seems like.

At eight o'clock Haustig Neefeld stands up, goes to the mike and starts to tell us what this meeting is for, that it is to pick those people who will go to Ottawa from Gutenthal to pick the new PC leader who will for sure be the next PM. For sure that's what the country needs, a PCPM, and Fuchtich Froese who is sitting there in the front starts to clap but the people don't clap, they start to shout, "We want Yeeat Shpanst!" And it looks like Haustig Neefeld doesn't know what to do, because for sure I'll bet he doesn't know who Yeeat Shpanst is any more than I do. So he stands there letting the people shout and he drinks some water and he still doesn't know what to do till Fuchtich Froese stands up and fuschels something in his ear. Then Haustig Neefeld lifts his arms up and spreads them out like wings holding his palms down and he shakes them up and down till the people get quiet and he says in a voice that squeaks a little bit like he is maybe telling a lie, "Ladies and Gentlemen. I give you Yeeat Shpanst!" Clapping and whistling and shouting for about five minutes and nothing happens. Then all of a sudden it feels like the people are making room for somebody in the middle of the rink. Everybody gets still. Then somebody is standing there in front by the mike. A short man, maybe five two, with a big baseball farmer cap on. He lifts his arms and points the visor of his cap to all the four corners of the curling rink. I hear a bobby pin drop out of Oata's hair. It sure is still. The man leans close to the mike.

"Welcome to the nineteen eighties!" You can hear five hundred people swallow their spit all through the rink.

"Welcome to this packed meeting!" Someplace one hand claps.

"Welcome to Yeeat Shpanst country!" Two hands clap.

"Welcome to Gutenthal!" A thousand hands clap, but quietly like if we were maybe in church.

"Ladies and Gentlemen. The bottom line, at this point in time, is between a rock and a hard place. Irregardless—irregardless of how you are politically orientated there's no doubt that the powers that be—the powers that shall no longer be—have impacted on every aspect of our lives with its metrificated Intrudo policies that are turning good people into confused objects of pity. Like my neighbor who was filling out a long government form last week and he had to convert all his bushels into litres and his acres into what-the-hecks." Somebody coughs. Somebody laughs a bit.

"Exactly. The trouble with our country today...." He stops and sips a bit of water. "The trouble with our country today is that our government in Ottawa is like a beetweeder that hacks off all the beets and leaves the weeds standing, then says, 'Look how well the crop is growing.' I say that it's time to let the government know that it is buttered out!" We clap now. Buttered out is good Flat German.

"Seriously now...." We still clap. "Thank you, thank you...." We clap harder. "Seriously now, the number one issue in the country today is the arrogance of incompetence that has turned our mighty Parliament into a house of ill repute—a common bawdy house!" We clap a little, but now we are a little nervous. I mean, should a Flat German talk like this?

"My friends, I did not come here to lick your recessionary wounds. In the past few weeks you have been inundated by known and unknown quantities asking for your support. Ladies and Gentlemen. I'm an unknown quantity, too. That's the monkey on my back. But it's the unknown that this country is yearning for in these troubled times. Who needs a track record—of derailments? Just consider the facts. This great party has been leaderless now for three months, and yet the polls show that our party has the highest popular standing in history. This is no time to cut our losses—just our losers. It is time to be forging ahead! The future is up for grabs! It is no time to back off!

"We must end this dramatic stalemate. We can no longer tolerate government by budget leak. Fellow Canadians, I stand before you offering to lead.

"But I am not alone. Others make the same offer. You deserve more. You deserve a real alternative. It has been said many times that there is no real difference between the two main parties in this country—except for arrogance. I propose to change all that.

"What this country needs is a new vision. I was born on a Manitoba sugar beet field. My earliest memories are of my dear mother's cracked and calloused heel as I learned to crawl along a row of beets. I lived in the granaries with the beetweeders. Yes, my native brothers, I was there with you. I watched my mother destroy the weeds. I watched the point of the hoe blade slip between double plants to cut off one so the other would have room to flourish. But look at the field today. The weeds grow alongside the beets, and whenever the beets get a little ahead of the weeds the government pumps more fertilizer on the weeds and when that isn't good enough it sends in Revenue Canada with hoes to cut down the best plants to give the weeds a better chance.

"I have a vision—I see millions of beetweeders with hoes sharpened descending on our choking fields, hacking away at the mustard and the wild oats, separating the doubles, freeing the sweet sugar beet to flourish as we weed our way into the future. There with the help of God I will lead you!"

And then before the people can even start to clap, Yeeat Shpanst shouts out that we should all sing "Oh, Canada" and that his campaign manager will lead us and a tall man in a blue suit jumps up beside him and starts to sing and it only takes one line before I know and everybody else knows that the singer is Hova Jake! Hova Jake whom I haven't seen since he went away to Rosthern College to school and then we heard one time that he was singing with a born again disco band. Well, for sure "Oh, Canada" sings hartsoft good.

For the next month Gutenthal is not the same. There are raffles, mission sales and collections to send Yeeat Shpanst to the leadership in Ottawa. All of a sudden it seems like he is relatives with almost everybody and he talks on CFAM and CISV and then one day he is even talking on CFRY. The *Echo* and *The Times* and *The Carillon* all have pictures of him and long writeups about what he says in his speeches. And always his meetings are packed with people, especially after Hova Jake brings along a quackgrass band that sings Flat German songs. Every evening we all watch *The Journal* to see if they will have heard of Yeeat Shpanst yet but it seems like Barbara and Mary Lou only know about the people whose initials are BM or JC, and when one of those JC guys makes it sound like the JC should remind us about a fisher of men, well the Gutenthallers think for sure that Yeeat Shpanst is the right man.

Haustig Neefeld, Fuchtich Froese, and Penzel Panna are the delegates from Gutenthal to Ottawa and seven days before the convention they crawl into one of those Triple E camper vans with Yeeat Shpanst and Hova Jake. Before he closes the door Yeeat says to those seeing him off, "In seven days we will change the world." Off they drive, and each day we listen to the radio and look at the television to see if we can hear about them, but there is nothing. Nothing at all. And we figure, well they'll be on TV for sure Friday night when all the candidates are supposed to make speeches. We all watch the TV on Friday night. And all the candidates make their speeches, but not Yeeat Shpanst. Nobody says even one word about him, not one word. We watch the TV till our eyes are sore trying to see the Gutenthallers someplace in the corner of the screen, and we think maybe we should have had another raffle so the quackgrass band could have gone along and for sure they would have gotten on TV.

Saturday all day, watching the TV. Sunday nobody goes to church in case something comes up on the TV, but nothing, nothing about Yeeat Shpanst. Not one person holding up a Yeeat Shpanst picture on a stick, not one. Where is he? Where are Haustig Neefeld and Fuchtich Froese?

I think maybe Penzel Panna got lost in a beer parlor because his wife isn't along to lead him by the nose.

So the PCs vote in somebody else, it doesn't really matter, and the Gutenthallers are thinking they should vote Social Credit again. I figure I'll just stick with the NDP. Monday afternoon Ha Ha Nickel gets a phone call from the Winnipeg airport to see if he will come to pick up Neefeld, Froese and Panna. So Ha Ha picks them up. Yeeat Shpanst and Hova are not along. The three men don't want to say nothing about what happened.

But one day I see Penzel Panna in town and I talk him into sneaking in the beer parlor with me and he tells me that the first thing that happened when they got to the convention was that Yeeat and Hova saw this hartsoft beautiful woman and somebody said that she writes for a newspaper. Yeeat and Hova right away went to her and said who they were and how they came there with the Triple E van and everything. So she said she would like to see the van to write about for her newspaper. They went outside to the van and the other three men were hungry and helping themselves to some sandwiches on a table. When they finished eating they turned to look for Yeeat Shpanst but they couldn't find him, even when they went back to the parking place. The van wasn't there. They walked up and down that garage, all twenty floors, but no van. All day Saturday and Sunday neither Yeeat nor Hova showed up and that hartsoft beautiful girl that writes for a newspaper didn't come back neither. Haustig Neefeld found out from another newspaper man with a funny name like Fudderingham, or something like that, that the hartsoft beautiful woman's name was Barbara, only it's not the Barbara from TV because she still comes on *The Journal* almost every day.

So I've got my seeding done and the fields are greening quite nice. The bank closed up Pug Peters's farm and had an auction sale. Hingst Heinrichs and the Farmers Revivalists wanted to do something about it and I even went to their meeting to say what I thought they should do: "Don't buy nothing at the auction sale!" Well, at the sale it seemed like that was the way it would be for a while, but then one guy saw what a good deal he could get there on a new swather so he started the bidding and before the day was over it seemed like just about everybody had bought something except me. Even I almost put in a bid for Pug's television dish but then I thought that if I brought home a $2,000 antenna they wouldn't be satisfied with that 11-inch black and white no more and be after me to buy color, and that's just too much. In these troubled times you have to watch out.

ADELE WISEMAN

from *Old Markets, New World*

When we were strangers in the land we made our own welcome and warmed ourselves with our own laughter and created our own belonging. To us the market-place was the least strange of all; there had always been markets.

I was a child then. For me the market was a place of looming backsides, off which we children caromed as off the padded walls of a roller-skating-rink. People were always bending over, searching in barrels, reaching, fingering. There was constant movement, arms and legs shooting out to be bumped into, people carrying things and shouting, 'Excuse me,' and 'Out of the way, little girl!'

From above, odd gifts would come, dropping with a benevolent 'Here, taste,' or drifting unescorted, like the handful of corn-hair, green and damp, that the farmer's wife flung down impatiently as she shucked the corn to prove to her customer that it was really golden bantam. 'Here, count yourself. Eight rows. Lovely corn.' She turned the golden cob triumphantly while I, watching, wound the cool hair round my fingers and put it to my nose.

To us below, identity smelled loud as voices. The crushed and trodden leaves and over-ripe fruit exhaled vigorous assertions, like echoes of the cries of the stall-keepers above.

'Tomatoes!' cried the man above. 'Fresh garden tomatoes! Man-i-toba bee-ooties!'

'Crushed tomato!' echoed the ground around his stall. 'I am a crushed tomato!'

'Cucumbers!' cried the farmer. 'Firm sweet cucumbers!'

'Leaky!' sang the stench below. 'I am a leaky hollow cucumber! Give me a kick and I'll smash apart!'

'Herring! Best schmaltz herring!' the man cajoled, above.

'Herring-barrel drippings; step in and smell worse than a wet and beshitten dog!' sang the world below, to which we children and the wasps and flies and dogs belonged.

Market people smelled too, of many smells, of sour cheese, of hay, of watermelon, of old clothes not for sale. And grandmothers smelled, grandmothers sitting on orange-crates, musty old grandmothers whose faces cracked into a thousand responsive wrinkles when you greeted them with 'Hello Bobeh.' Sometimes one of them drew you close for a pat on the head. She smelled as a grandmother who sits swathed in dresses and sweaters and coat and shawl and woollen stockings and ankle boots in all weathers can be expected to smell—inoffensively unrefreshing.

....

A subtle change took place in the relationship between seller and customer in the evening. The customer was no longer in a hurry to get home to make lunch or supper. It was the stall man who was anxious to make his sales and be gone. Limp, picked-over merchandise was offered at drastically reduced prices. You didn't have to haggle so much. 'All right, take it, take it. Cut my heart out.' The free tragic performance that came with the goods was also a little tired by the time evening came, for sincerity was tempered, on the part of the actor, by the knowledge that he was getting rid of something that would be unfit for sale and a dead loss tomorrow.

There were other reasons why young immigrants liked a stroll through the market in the evening, after work, reasons implied in the stories we heard so often, about how she met him in the market and he bought her a bag of chips and carried home her watermelon.

'Can you eat such a big watermelon all by yourself?'

'No, it's really for my landlady and her family.'

'And who's your landlady?'

And it turned out that the landlady's brother-in-law came from the same town in the old country as this young man, which made practically a blood tie, soon to be cemented in a happy marriage, with the landlady's childless brother-in-law helping out the young man to such an extent that they were now practically rich and the watermelon girl hardly spoke to any of her old market acquaintances any more. Success stories often ended in this ambiguous way, but that didn't seem to deter anyone from dreaming.

If we were lucky, we children were taken along to help shop for the weekly chicken. Picking the Sabbath fowl is a serious affair, too serious to be accomplished without much deliberation. First you run your eyes over the clucking coop until they light on an attractive bird. Ask to have a look at her. Take her firmly by the legs. Feel her breast for signs of scrawniness. She must have a good, healthy deposit of white meat. Up-end her and blow into her rear downfeathers to see if the skin beneath reveals a good blush of yellow fat. Give her an extra feel to make sure. Some women even go so far as to insert an expert finger to find out if they'll be getting an egg into the bargain. It's an intricate, intimate business getting to know your fowl, and it is not surprising that the unlucky bird, who has been man-handled, up-ended, and outright violated, lets out a protesting squawk sometimes and madly flaps her wings. But she is soon subdued, and submits in baffled, glaring silence, her red-shot amber eyes fixed in angry resignation.

Once our bird was chosen and paid for she was hauled off to the slaughter shack. Well we children knew that here in this little shack, from which came the desperate squawks of 'Help! Help!' the awesome business of the hallowing of the slaughter of food was taking place. As we waited outside we exchanged gory stories about what was going on inside, dared each other to peek in, and wondered whether this was going to be one of those legendary birds who would go on flapping and squawking and jumping around the shack for three hours after its throat had been slit. An uneasy silence fell upon us as we heard from within the shack the ultimate, unavailing cry of tomorrow's boiled chicken hurled into what, but for us, was an indifferent universe.

While we waited for the chicken-plucker to be finished plucking feathers and singeing lice we discussed questions of humane slaughter. Was our way of killing food better than 'their' way? Well I should say so! Mostly they just grabbed a chicken by the neck and whirled it round and round to break its neck, poor little thing. Or sometimes they chopped its head off, so there was a red gushy stump left. But even if they only put a bullet in it, it was a pretty messy, unholy way to kill, without even a prayer or anything.

Sometimes, as we grew older, we decided that no way for a chicken to die could be condoned and vowed we wouldn't eat tomorrow's boiled chicken, ever again, not for anything. But there is a magician lurking in the most unassuming mother, who can undo the ardour of even the highest youthful principle. All she has to hear is the trembly, indignant little speech about how you will refuse to eat the meat of this cruelly murdered chicken, and tomorrow, instead of the same old boiled Sabbath fowl you will find a transformation on the table, a metamorphosis, roasted and stuffed and with a salivary allure quite unrelated to the bird whose immolation you swore to remember the day before.

....

Those were the early years. The time came, one summer, when I went to work in the market myself, to earn my college fees. My boss was a tall, stooping old man who spat a lot. Our tiny hutch was adjacent to the old Winnipeg Farmers' Market. It was a fruit shop, so small you had to pull in your stomach to make room when more than two customers came in at the same time. The rough, wooden floor was all black and oily from ground-in old gob and squashed fruit-leavings, which it was my job to sweep up in my spare time, when the old man went and sat on a bench outside to gossip with his cronies, and the dim-lit box in which I worked was for a moment free of the squeezers, the hagglers, and the other potential customers, whom he regarded at one and the same time as the providers and despoilers of his livelihood.

All day long—and a long, long day it was—we circled our small domain, checking the boxes and the crates and refilling the cartons and the baskets. Here we nipped a brown leaf, expertly, so it wouldn't show much; there we scraped with deft thumbnail at the first hint of coming mould. From the inside, I got a good close look at the life of anxiety bordering on anguish that is lived by the marginal traders of the perishable goods of the earth. With profit so small, with wastage so high, with the goods he is selling deteriorating by the minute before his very eyes, no wonder the storekeeper gives way sometimes to his gnawing wrath when customer after customer reaches out a greedy hand and in a few short hours a firm, nubile little tomato is turned into a bruised old pro. Every leaf to be discarded was a loss; every fruit or vegetable that a customer criticized was to be defended with peevish and despairing eloquence.

The little fruit shop is gone. The old market on Winnipeg's North Main has given way to a parking-lot and there are rumours of ambitious city plans for the area. The Farmers' Market, what's left of it, has been removed to an arid, antiseptic setting somewhere in the city's outskirts. My uncle doesn't do much business there any more. Nellie, of course, has long since gone where the good nags go, and I suppose it's just as well. Her turd would look out of place on the immaculate asphalt parking semicircle round which the farmers' stalls are neatly ranged.

. . . .

There are lovely old markets in Canada still, and peddlers who still sit on their wagons behind blinkered old nags. But the horses are disappearing and the markets are developing a kind of strangeness about them that is in addition to the strangeness they once had as places where immigrants gathered and practised feeling at home. It is the strangeness of the past persistent, the past persisting into a future which probably has no place for it. Not long ago some friends introduced me to the Kensington Market in Toronto. For me it had all the fun and excitement and good warmth and the feeling of belonging in my life that I have looked for and found in markets all over the globe. But most of the market dealers were of a generation that is gradually passing away. And the customers were mainly fairly recent immigrants and those of us who like to drop in on the past, occasionally, when we have time.

But if the markets, as we knew them, are doomed to disappear some day, the old market men will be the last to mourn. They did not bring up their sons to stand all day long in the cold, blowing on freezing knuckles, nor to stand wiping the steam from their eyes in the day-long heat. 'Thank God,' remarked one old man, 'my sons don't have to make a living this way. Thank God,' he repeated, as he stood among the bottles and other junk treasures outside his shop, his hands in his pockets, far from elegantly dressed but nevertheless the picture of a successful man. 'You know, every day I thank God,' he added, 'and especially I thank him for three things. I thank him for my years, for my health, and for my little bit of money in the bank.'

We paused at a stall set up in front of an old Toronto house of the kind that it is fashionable for young, artistic people to dream about buying up cheap, and 'doing things with,' a house decrepit, but with all kinds of 'interesting potential if the right people got hold of it.' I asked the vendor, an elderly, frail-looking man, 'Do you live in that house?'

He was indignant. 'You want I should live in a house like that?'

No, they have their own dreams in the market-place, and you can see them still, the dream-filled eyes of young women brooding over what is to come and the doom-drowned eyes of their grandmothers brooding over where it went to. That old man who looks like the head of the Russian government may be dreaming about the statesmanlike qualities he has already discovered in his grandson, or he may be deciding, 'Let him own a supermarket if he doesn't want to be a doctor,' about that little boy, half-a-hip high, to whom all of life is still a dream to come.

Once, recently, when I was wandering through the limbo of a Montreal supermarket, pushing my cart up and down the long, lonely aisles, picking up packages and putting them down again, calculating sizes of cartons, adding up ounces against conflicting prices, unable to come to any conclusion about who was trying to gyp me more and unable to find a human being who cared enough to fight it out with, I had an odd experience. I was reaching into the milk-products display case which runs along the entire width of the back of the store, when a shopping-cart was driven firmly into the small of my back, pinning me against the refrigerator.

'Would you mind, while you're down there, to reach me a package of cheese?' asked a little old lady, dressed in a fashionable fur coat, with her gloved hands quite firmly maintaining their pressure on the shopping-cart.

When I complied she looked at the neat, glassy package with disgust, and I could see in her eyes the memories of great damp slabs from which the stall women would give you tasters before they cut with a big knife, unerringly, the amount you wanted. But she thanked me politely and I continued on my way. A moment later I was again nudged by the shopping-cart. Again I was asked to reach for something and again I complied. When I had done so she proceeded to drive me along the entire length of the refrigerator, pinned to the front rim of her shopping-cart, as though I were trapped on one of those cow-catchers they used to have on trains. She directed me with a nudge, now on this hip, now on that, now appearing beside, now behind, now with a little racing movement in front, to bar my way and ask me if I'd reach for something, or read the small print on the package because she couldn't see very well. Neither her reflexes nor her eyesight were poor enough to prevent her from spotting any move I made to escape and scotching it with a clever twist of the steering bar. I had the distinct impression that she was surreptitiously putting back everything I dutifully handed her, for all my bending and fetching didn't seem to add much to her cart.

But as she drove me along in front of her I felt a strong conviction that I knew who this old lady was. Her children had peeled off the layers of clothes, of sweaters and skirts and wool stockings and ankle boots. They had bought her a fur coat, through which it is hard to perceive dry-old-lady smell, and exchanged her kerchief for a hat with a feather; they had parked her in an apartment up-town, away from her old friends and the market life that she knew; but I recognized her. And I began to wonder if perhaps she had not recognized something in me, too, in this cold place.

Finally, I turned and put my hand restrainingly on her shopping-cart. 'I have to go now,' I said, as gently as I could. On an impulse I added, 'Good-bye, Bobeh.'

For an instant I caught the gleam that precedes the cracking-up of an old lady's face into a thousand smiling wrinkles. Then she glanced round quickly, a puzzled expression gathering up the mobile wrinkles. Her eyes sought my face with an anxious scrutiny. 'Do I know you, daughter?' she whispered, finally.

I felt a pang for having upset her. 'I used to know you in the market,' I lied.

The wrinkles righted themselves slowly to a smile. 'Rachel Street?' she said. 'That's a market. There at least you can say a word to someone. Not like this.' Her gesture took in the whole new world of supermarkets and shopping centres.

'Yes,' I agreed. 'Yes.'

'Still,' she added thoughtfully. 'It's a good business.' And she sighed.

EROTH

Manitoba Poem

In Manitoba, a farmer will prepare
for spring and contrary to popular notion
women are not foremost in men's
minds: the new warmth has made them
aware of trains and hills, of things
that would make them leave women completely:
something else keeps them. And the women
are just as glad for the rest.

Summer comes in from Saskatchewan on
a hot and rolling wind. Faces
burnt and forearms burnt, the men seed
their separate earths and listen to the CBC
for any new report of rain. Each day now
the sun is bigger and from the kitchen
window, it sets a mere hundred feet behind
the barn, where a rainbow once came down.

Four months later this is over, men
are finished. Children return
to school and catch colds in their
open jackets. Women prepare
for long nights under 6-inch goosedown
quilts. Outside, the trees shake off
their leaves as if angered by the new
colours. And without any more warning than
this, winter falls on the world,
taking no one by surprise. No one.

The Hunters of the Deer

The ten men will dress in white
to match the snow and leave the last
farmhouse and the last woman, going
north into the country of the deer. It
is from there, and from past there, that
the wind begins that can shake
every window in the house and leaves
the woman wishing she had moved away
five years and five children ago.

During the day the father of her children
will kill from a distance. With the others
he will track and drive each bush
and at least once he will kill before
they stop and come together for
coffee in scratched quart jars. And
sometimes the November sun will glint
on the rifles propped together in the snow.

In the evening, as they skin and gut,
they talk about the one that ran three
miles on a broken leg and the bitch wolf
they should have shot and how John
the bachelor likes eating more than
hunting and they pass the whiskey
around to keep warm. In the house
the woman makes a meal from pork.

These men are hunters and later,
standing in bright electrically lighted
rooms they are embarrassed with the
blood on their clothes and although the
woman nods and seems to understand,
she grows restless with their talk.
She has not heard another woman in fourteen days.

And when they leave, the man sleeps
and his children sleep while the woman
waits and listens for the howling of
wolves. To the north, the grey
she-wolf smells the red snow and howls.
She also is a hunter of the deer.
Tonight, while other hunters sleep, she
drinks at the throat.